T0005900

More Acclaim for *Leading with Aloha*

"Every educator has a story, and Jan Iwase has shared her story in *Leading with Aloha*. Jan has always led with heart, which is vitally important for any school leader because it elevates our impact. *Leading with Aloha* lets us all in on where that heartfelt leadership began and offers us important lessons into how we should all lead our schools."
—Peter DeWitt, EdD, consultant and author, "Finding Common Ground" *(Education Week)*

"New teachers and principals would do well to put Jan's little book at the top of their reading lists. Part memoir, part lessons learned, *Leading with Aloha* offers both wisdom and insightful inspiration from a veteran of 45 years in public education."
—Dan Boylan, author, *MidWeek* columnist, Emeritus Professor of History, University of Hawai'i–West O'ahu

"As a long–time fellow educator, a military spouse, and the mother of four children who attended Hale Kula Elementary School where Jan was the principal, I can bear witness to the fact that she truly leads with aloha, thus setting the tone for teachers, staff, and students alike. Jan's story provides a window into the journey that made her one of the individuals and educators I admire most."
—Julia Myers, EdD, math educator and consultant

"Take a journey into the 45-year career of an amazing educator who captures the essence of how reflecting on personal and professional experiences impacts your core values and beliefs. In *Leading with Aloha* Jan shares her roots growing up in the plantation era of Hawai'i and how the values learned led her to a career in education—a career that took her from the classroom as an early childhood teacher to her final 15 years as a principal. This book made me ponder how one becomes a great leader and gave me insight into how Jan became a great leader. But it especially made me reflect on my own experiences and how those experiences have shaped me."
—Chad Keone Farias, Complex Area Superintendent, East Hawai'i

Leading
with
Al🍍ha

From the Pineapple Fields
to the Principal's Office

Leading
with
Al ha

From the Pineapple Fields
to the Principal's Office

Jan Iwase

LEGACY ISLE
PUBLISHING

*Dedicated with aloha to
Jace and Jayden*

© 2019 Jan Iwase

All rights reserved. No part of this book may be reproduced in any form or by any electronic or mechanical means, including information retrieval systems, without prior written permission from the publisher, except for brief passages quoted in reviews.

ISBN 978-1-948011-17-4

Library of Congress Control Number: 2019941527

A portion of the proceeds from sales of this book support the National Kidney Foundation of Hawaiʻi.

Design and production
Ingrid Lynch

Background images on front cover and pp. 21, 57 and 99: iStock/jammydesign.
Front cover illustration, center: iStock/Lyubchik Prokopchuk.
Front cover illustration, bottom: iStock/izumikobayashi.
All other photos from Jan Iwase.

Legacy Isle Publishing
1000 Bishop St., Ste. 806
Honolulu, HI 96813
Toll-free 1-866-900-BOOK
info@legacyislepublihsing.net
www.legacyislepublishing.net

10 9 8 7 6 5 4 3 2

Printed in Korea

Contents

ACKNOWLEDGMENTS

Writing this book was a huge endeavor, necessitating numerous edits and revisions which required commitment, perseverance, and patience. This book would not have been possible without the guidance and support from many people, and I would like to acknowledge and thank them:

• Denise Murai, Yuuko Arikawa, Rick Tsujimura, Anne Amemiya, Carmen Pita, Michelle Lau, and our son Justin read my drafts, asked questions for clarification, and made suggestions for improvement.

• My brother, Chris, not only read several drafts and made suggestions, he also agreed to write the foreword.

• Peter DeWitt, Cris Waldfogel, Eric Sheninger, Julia Myers, Dan Boylan, and Chad Keone Farias wrote testimonials; I am grateful for their support for this project.

• George Engebretson from Legacy Isle Publishing encouraged and navigated me through this whole process to get this, my first book, published. He helped me greatly.

• Our son Jordan as well as my mom and my siblings provided moral support and encouragement throughout this project.

• Finally, my husband, Randy, was by my side from beginning to end. His questions and reminders to think about the "person at the bus stop," who may not be familiar with educational jargon, helped bring coherence to my manuscript.

FOREWORD

For as long as I can remember, my sister Jan wanted to become an educator. A tireless advocate and champion for children and their education, she has always been an inspiration to me, and I am immensely proud of her for writing this memoir. I've seen her rise from our humble beginnings on a pineapple plantation in rural Hawai'i, to become a State-recognized teacher and principal. If you're like me, you'll be shaking your head in amazement by her grit and determination as she went along her journey and how she never lost sight of her overarching goal of being an educator—to assure that each and every student was given an opportunity to learn. Educators are overworked, underappreciated, and underpaid, yet they are the most influential forces in our lives outside of our parents. In this book Jan chronicles her journey and the way her life's experiences informed how she became a better, more compassionate, resourceful, and engaging educator.

I can fondly remember the very first Head Start classroom in which my sister taught, a tiny room that was part of a Buddhist church. To me, it was a rundown, dingy room with dirty windows, dusty cement floors, and an out-of-tune spinet piano in the corner. But for Jan, it was her chance to finally show her mettle as a teacher. She transformed that room(!), and she transformed the students and their parents, who were grateful to have their kids in such a positive learning environment. I visited her class a few times and it warmed my heart to see just how dedicated she was and how engaged and participatory she made her students and parents. I guess I knew way back then that she would go on to great things in her life as an educator.

Flash forward to more modern times and we can see that being an educator today is nothing like it was when Jan and my other siblings and I were growing up. Long gone are the days when teachers taught and when students were expected to sit in their seats and listen. Today, there is no one correct modality for teaching, and creativity and resourcefulness in getting the students to learn and become lifelong learners is more the norm. Jan's own experiences led her to discover early on that students learn and retain more when learning is interactive and fun. This helped usher in project- and inquiry-based group discussions well before they had become buzzwords in today's education environment. In university classrooms today, including the introductory biology classes that I teach, we are now adopting such creative "active" and "peer-to-peer" learning methods, and education research studies have borne out that these methods are superior to traditional "passive" learning. As a principal, Jan encouraged her teachers to try new ways to click with their students and to foster their development as lifelong learners. She discusses the need for this flexibility at length and how modern technology should be embraced, where appropriate, in today's classroom.

It is fitting that Jan has mentioned her husband of 42 years, Randy, as an integral part of her life story. When we were first introduced to Randy, we weren't sure what to make of him. You see, he was a city boy—boisterous, comedic, and unafraid to speak his mind on all manner of topics. We were all a bit afraid that she was in over her head, being the shy "country" girl to his "townie" sophisticated persona. But over time it was clear that she was the ying to his yang and they made a great pair, with her quiet but persuasive demeanor winning out on many issues, including where they ended up living (close to our parents!) and from where he would launch his political career. It isn't easy being a spouse of a politician and maintaining a full-time job, not to mention having to take over the lion's share of child care. We were heartened to see that Jan decided to become a principal once Randy retired from his political career, and that, in turn, he supported her decision to serve in a crucial administrative capacity. They make a great pair and raised three wonderfully thoughtful and compassionate sons with the best characteristics of both of them. Throughout their professional lives, Jan and Randy chose paths that put them in the service of others, and, consequently, have touched the lives of countless people over the years.

Readers of this book who have not lived in Hawai'i may not be so familiar with the deeper meaning of the term, "aloha." Aloha is more than just a way to say hello or goodbye. It is a way of life, a mantra ensconced into the fabric of Hawai'i that roughly translates to feelings of hope and pride, goodwill, warmth and love. It is pervasive and people in Hawai'i practice it on a daily basis. My sister's conveyance of aloha in the classroom is particularly apropos when dealing with foreign and military-impacted students, both of whom are found in large numbers in certain Hawai'i schools. These students often lack a sense of belonging, and trying to find a shared humanity through aloha helps to ease their transition and assimilation. I think we could all use more aloha in our lives.

—Chris T. Amemiya, PhD
Professor of Molecular and Cellular Biology
University of California, Merced

Introduction

It has been a wonderful journey! Back in 1973, I was a bright-eyed, optimistic, somewhat naive 21-year-old, ready to take on the world after obtaining my teaching degree. I spent 45 years in education, and I never regretted my decision. I loved kids and I enjoyed school, so it was a perfect career choice for me. Teaching is challenging, and I greatly respect those who have made a commitment to this profession. As an educator, my goal was to instill a joy of learning in our students and staff, and to help them to realize their potential.

I have lived in Hawai'i for my whole life. Hawai'i is a state with a unique history and culture. We have eight main islands, each with their own special features. We are the only state that was once ruled by a monarchy. At one time, pineapple and sugar were the major industries, and immigrants were hired to provide the labor. This led to Hawai'i being a melting pot of cultures. Being surrounded by the Pacific Ocean means that we are strategically located between the continental United States and Asia; hence, the military has a major presence on our island. Here in Hawai'i, the concept of aloha permeates what we do and how we treat others. It is more than just a greeting; it is a way of life. It means that we respect our island home and the people who live here. As I reflect on my career, I realize that choosing to lead with aloha—love, compassion, empathy, and respect—was what drove me to do my best for our students and our school community throughout my career.

My motivation for writing this book was not to tell others how to be a teacher or a principal. Rather, it is to encourage readers to reflect on the personal and professional experiences that have impacted the core values and beliefs that influence them today. This knowledge directly affects how we interact with others and how we lead, whether it is in a classroom or at a school or in some other capacity in our lives. I know that my humble roots growing up in my family in a pineapple plantation community shaped me. With five children in our household, I learned to assert myself when necessary, but I also learned to compromise. I learned to listen to the opinions of others and to be empathetic to their feelings. I learned that love and encouragement can make a difference in how we react to challenges. I learned to accept disappointment but to never give up on my goals. These experiences directly impacted why I chose to lead with aloha.

My professional experiences also influenced me. I have a special place in my heart for my first students, all of whom were from low-income families. Their parents, knowing how important a preschool experience could be, committed to team with us at Head Start so their children would benefit. We worked together—home and school—to give these students the confidence and the skills to be successful in kindergarten and beyond. My heart was filled with aloha for these preschoolers. They may have been from underprivileged homes, but their parents were determined that their children would have better opportunities in life than they had, just like my parents did for my siblings and me.

As a principal at our military-impacted school, leading with aloha was essential. It wasn't unusual for students to be uprooted during the school year to move to Hawai'i and for the military parent to be preparing for deployment shortly after arriving on-island. It isn't easy to be the new kid in the class again, to have to make new friends again, and to learn different routines and procedures again. By showing aloha to our new students and families, we were sharing what makes Hawai'i a special place, and I felt that this could have a lasting impact on them. I believe that our military students are the best possible ambassadors for our Hawai'i schools. It was always my hope that after leaving our school, they would have the confidence to share the spirit of aloha wherever their path might take them in the future.

All of my personal and professional experiences molded me to be the kind of educator I wanted for my own children and grandchildren. As a society, I believe it is our responsibility to make this world a better place for the next generation, and that was always my goal as an educator. I constantly remind myself of a Native American proverb: "We don't inherit this earth from our ancestors; we borrow it from our children." These words of wisdom influenced the decisions I made and how I chose to lead with aloha.

This book is organized into three parts. The first part shares my life journey, the people, and the experiences that shaped my views and thinking. In the second part, I share my core values and beliefs that helped me to lead with aloha—it all began in Whitmore Village, a small plantation community in Wahiawā, Oʻahu, Hawaiʻi. The last chapter is a tribute to our son, Jarand, who passed away on May 20, 2018, from chronic kidney disease. It is a reminder to all of us to take better care of ourselves so we can be there for others. I am sure Jarand is proud of his mom for taking a step out of her comfort zone to write a book about her experiences and what she learned in her 45 years as an educator.

This journey was not mine alone. My parents, Keiji and Vivian Amemiya, gave me the roots and wings to be successful on this 45-year adventure. My husband, Randy, was at my side, encouraging me and listening to my excitement as well as my concerns and challenges through 42 of those 45 years. Our sons, Justin, Jarand, and Jordan, were my best "subjects," always willing to help me become a better educator by letting me test new ideas with them and helping me to understand that all children are different, and they are all special. Everyone who touched my life has played a part in molding me into the educator and the leader I became. My journey began in Whitmore Village and included all those who taught me, who taught with me, and who became my school ʻohana. I am grateful to them all.

Thank you for this opportunity to share my experiences and my thoughts about leading with aloha. ✿

PART ONE

MY LIFE EXPERIENCES

"I am part of all that I have met…"
—*"Ulysses," Alfred, Lord Tennyson*

Roots and Wings

"There are two things children should get
from their parents: roots and wings."
—*Johann Wolfgang von Goethe*

Roots

They say it takes a village to raise a child. In my case, that is true. I grew up in Whitmore Village, a small plantation community north of Wahiawā, Hawai'i. Driving to or from the beaches on the North Shore, one would likely miss the entrance to our village, surrounded as it was by pineapple fields. Growing up in Whitmore Village taught me values such as perseverance, respect and caring for others, kindness, trust, and humility. These values continue to influence me today.

Most of the residents at that time were of Japanese or Filipino ancestry, and they were laborers, working in the fields or doing other jobs in the pineapple industry. It was hard work and didn't pay much, but it was what families had to do to make a living, and they did so without complaining. Because of their sacrifices, many of my generation were able to go to college and get jobs that did not require the backbreaking labor that our parents and their ancestors endured.

Our whole world was in that village. Our grandparents and other relatives lived in Whitmore. We went to school there. We played there. We even shopped there at Whitmore Supermarket, owned by the Matsumoto family. If we needed something—bread, eggs, luncheon meat—my mom would send us to the store. The Matsumotos knew that plantation families struggled to make ends meet, so if we didn't have cash to pay, the clerks would write down what we bought and how much we owed, and the next payday, the bill would be paid off. They did this for all the Whitmore families. I remember when Foodland opened a store in Wahiawā, which was the closest town to us. The store was huge and much less personal than at Matsumoto Store where the clerks probably knew every adult and child who came in to make a purchase.

My parents never spoke about the hardships and challenges they endured growing up. Our ancestors left Japan to work as contract laborers in Hawai'i in order to make a better life for their families. They knew it would not be an easy life, but their belief in "*kodomo no tame ni*" gave them the determination to work hard and keep going "for the sake of the children." I know how tirelessly our parents and ancestors worked and sacrificed in order to give us opportunities they never had.

Our ancestors also brought with them a resiliency based on "*shikata ga nai.*" Rather than wringing their hands over perceived challenges or injustices, they lived by the belief that "it cannot be helped." Our parents were great examples of living this belief, passed on by those who came before them. My dad, as the oldest of seven children, left high school at age 15 to work as a laborer at Hawaiian Pineapple Company (later Dole Corporation) to help his family financially. I remember Dad's mom, Grandma Amemiya, telling me that a teacher came to the house, begging her not to let Dad quit school because she saw so much potential in him, but the decision had already been made. My dad, as the oldest, had a responsibility to help out the family. Because of Dad's unselfish sacrifice, all of his sisters and brothers completed high school, and his brothers both graduated from college.

Mom had two older brothers, and when she was about two years old, her mother passed away during childbirth. Her Grandma Waka came to live with them to take care of the family and to help with the household. When I speak with Mom about growing up in her formative years without a mother, she says it's just the way it was and the family made the best of the situation. As a fourth-generation Japanese American, I owe much to my parents and my ancestors. They instilled in me the values that we now pass on to our children and grandchildren.

Dad started off as a laborer at the pineapple company and steadily worked his way up to become a superintendent. In those early days, though, workers only got paid if they worked. If the weather was bad, the horn did not blow at the designated time in the morning, indicating that work that day was canceled. This was a hardship, especially for many young families, and emphasizes why the village was so important. People helped each other by sharing homegrown fruits and vegetables or fresh fish they caught. Matsumoto Store was a lifeline during those times of inclement weather as they extended credit to families, knowing that it might take longer for them to repay their debts.

Mom attended business college after high school and got a job at Hawaiian Pineapple Company after graduating. She met Dad at work, and they dated then got married in 1949. The babies came shortly after—Corinne first, then me, Debbie next, Roy fourth, and finally, Chris. Mom had her hands full, taking care of the kids and the household. At one time, there were four of us who were five years old and younger! It wasn't until Chris was older and we sisters could babysit that Mom went back to work.

It must have been challenging to raise five kids on one income, but we didn't realize it because our parents never complained. We lived in a small, old, two-bedroom cottage that my parents first rented for $35 per month, then bought from Hawaiian Pineapple Company for $5,000. Four of us slept in one bedroom, and my youngest brother slept with Mom and Dad. My parents, like so many of our neighbors and relatives, were resourceful. Dad always had a garden where he grew vegetables and fruits. He also loved fishing and diving, so we often had fresh fish and other seafood for dinner. At one time, Dad raised chickens, and our job as kids was to carefully collect the eggs and bring them into the house. Mom cooked whatever Dad raised or caught, and there was no complaining about not liking what was for dinner. We ate what was served. Mom made jams and jellies, and she also pickled vegetables from Dad's harvest of cabbage or won bok. We had a compost pit, and any food waste that couldn't be placed there was taken to our neighbor's slop can, and farmers came by weekly to collect the discarded food for their pigs. Mom knew that all the girls would have new dresses for school, so each summer, my sisters and I browsed through the Montgomery Ward or Sears Roebuck catalogues to find dresses we liked. Mom would then take our measurements, buy the material, draft the pattern pieces on newspaper, and sew new dresses for us. It wasn't until I started sewing that I realized how special these one-of-a-kind dresses were.

When I started kindergarten, a whole new world opened for me. I loved school! Most kids in our village didn't go to nursery school, so kindergarten was our first school experience. Helemano School was an old school in the middle of pineapple fields that my parents attended when they were little. My sister, Corinne, who is a year older than me, also attended school at that location for her kindergarten year. Luckily, when I started kindergarten, the school had been rebuilt right in our Whitmore community, so I walked to and from school every day, accompanied by Aunty Brenda and her friends who were in the eighth grade at that time. Kindergarten was not academic back then. Instead, it was an opportunity to make new friends, play cooperatively with others, learn to listen and follow instructions, and gain confidence. We had sharing time, played dress-up in the house corner, built with blocks, drew with crayons, and painted on easels. We learned new songs, and our teacher read us stories as we lay in our sleeping bags for nap time after lunch. It was while I was in kindergarten that I decided that I wanted to be a teacher when I grew up.

I learned about letters and numbers in grade one; I remember helping other students on a table outside the classroom. One thing, however, caused me a great deal of stress in first grade, and that was handwriting. I was young, probably the youngest in my class since I was born in December. I tried really hard to replicate those letters and numbers, but mine did not look like the teacher's. The grade on my report card reflected my poor fine motor coordination, and it was suggested that I needed to practice more at home. I couldn't go out to play until I practiced a page of letters or numbers or words. I remember how I hated being inside and often cried because when I tried to erase a letter or number, the thin newsprint paper would tear. Eventually, my fine motor coordination caught up with my peers, and my handwriting grade improved, but I will never forget the stress I felt at that time. Later when I became a teacher and a parent, I remembered how I felt, and it helped me to be understanding to those who just needed a little more time to develop, whatever the skill deficit.

Back then, learning about one's cultural background was important. I remember Whitmore *doshikai* parties where all the village families of Japanese ancestry gathered to eat, talk story, share their talents, and enter to win lucky number prizes. There was an annual Rizal Day picnic at the neighborhood park honoring a national hero from the Philippines, Jose Rizal. We watched from afar as boys tried to climb the greased flagpole, hoping to be the one to get the monetary prize at the top.

When I was old enough, I got on a bus after school and attended Wahiawa Gakuen where we were exposed to the language and culture of our ancestors. Until then, we rarely ever left our village, and I was a bit intimidated at first because Wahiawā seemed like a huge city. The teachers spoke very little English, and since I didn't speak Japanese, there was definitely a language barrier. The teachers read us stories in Japanese, and I remember trying to figure out what the story was about by looking at the pictures and listening to the teacher's inflection as she read the story. I didn't retain much of what I learned back then, and I regret not being able to speak or understand the language. My paternal grandpa, an *issei* or immigrant from Japan, spoke very little English, and I saw his frustration when we couldn't understand what he was trying to communicate to us. As a teacher, my experiences back then taught me that when students are English language learners, we need to provide instruction in multiple ways so they can begin to make connections. I also realize the sacrifices that our ancestors had to overcome when they chose to leave the comforts of their home to come to Hawai'i to work.

In time, our parents were able to save up enough to build a prefabricated Hicks Home in the back of our two-bedroom house. We definitely needed more room with five children in the family, and it was pretty exciting to have four bedrooms and a brand-new house! When a trailer came by to move the original house, we now had a spacious front yard. Back then we could play for hours with the neighborhood kids. We would play in our front yard or our driveway, or we would go to the park and play games like water or prisoner's base or sky inning. We even went hiking all by ourselves down the gulch to pick *liliko'i* (passion fruit) or guava. We'd pack a snack and a drink and bring along a bag for the fruit we gathered. When I look back, I cannot believe our parents allowed us to go down there by ourselves—but of course those were different times.

My family lived on a modest income. We were not financially wealthy, but we were rich in so many other ways. Throughout my growing-up years, our family spent a lot of time together. We went to the beach and stopped for shave ice afterwards. We went to cheer for my brothers when they played Little League games, and on weekends, we went to matinees at the Victory or Wahiawa Theaters to watch many of the Disney movies. At home, we played board or card games, and none of us liked to lose because we were so competitive. My dad was a good singer, but none of us inherited his voice; nevertheless, we loved singing especially on our trips around the island. Mom and Dad taught us songs from their day, and I in turn taught some of these songs to our sons and my students. These were things that did not cost much but made special memories for us kids.

All of us worked in the pineapple fields during the summer. It was a rite of passage. When we became of age, it was expected that we would work at least one summer picking pineapples. We needed to prove to ourselves that we could handle the physical and mental challenges to work in the fields, picking pineapples for a full workday. After all, this was what our ancestors did when they first came to Hawai'i. It was exhausting, but working in the pineapple fields for five summers taught me many lessons, especially about teamwork, resilience, perseverance, the value of hard work, and the importance of continuing my education if I wanted choices in my life.

When I was a senior in high school, my parents bought a home in Mililani in an area that was pineapple fields just a few years earlier. It was an opportunity to purchase a new home in a master-planned community that offered many amenities for families. Today, Mililani is a sprawling suburb with close to 50,000 residents. It is where Randy and I chose to raise our family, and we still live here. Dad passed away in 2013, but Mom continues to live in the home they bought back in 1969. She is 91 years young.

Growing up in Whitmore Village taught me so much about life. I learned about treating others with respect and about not giving up even when things were difficult. I learned that even if we come from humble roots, with the support and encouragement from others, we can achieve our goals. I learned to respect and appreciate other cultures. Most of all, I learned that there were people who cared about me and wanted me to succeed—my parents, my teachers, and others in Whitmore—and who were proud when someone from our village did well. I carried these lessons with me throughout my personal and professional life and strived to pass them on to my children and my students when I became a parent and a teacher.

WINGS

Education, giving back to our community, and a strong work ethic were emphasized in our family. We were expected to do our best in school and to make the most of our opportunities. Our parents often read to us from a dark purple set of books with stories, poems, and other literature. Roy remembers Mom making him read to her as she did her ironing. "Enunciate!" she commanded as she made him repeat what he read over and over. Those practices probably helped Roy today as he is required to speak to audiences ranging from intimate gatherings to large crowds in his job as City managing director. I remember taking the bus with Mom to borrow books at the Wahiawa Library or from the bookmobile that visited our community. Reading was something that was emphasized in our family, and it continues to be one of my favorite pastimes today.

I enjoyed my elementary school years. I was the kind of student who never had trouble or made trouble. After all, our parents would be disappointed if any of their children misbehaved in school. I loved reading and math, but I also loved music, physical education, and recess. I didn't like art much; I felt I wasn't very good compared to other students. What I realized years later when I became a teacher was that everyone has strengths, and we need to provide opportunities for each person to shine. I also realized that art, like writing, is a process; students should have opportunities to self-reflect, receive feedback, and revise their work. Too often, subjects like art, music, and physical education are swept to the side in our elementary school classrooms in favor of the academics. I sincerely hope this mindset changes so that all students have the opportunity to be exposed to a well-rounded education.

At the end of sixth grade, we got exciting news. We would be attending Wahiawa Intermediate School for seventh and eighth grade! It was a bit intimidating to go from our small community school where we knew everyone to attending a much larger school with students from all over Wahiawā, including those who lived at the Schofield and Wheeler military bases. I remember worrying about whether I would be able to keep up academically, but I soon realized that our teachers at Helemano School had prepared us well.

At Wahiawa Intermediate, we took classes such as music, art, physical education, home economics, typing, and communications in addition to the core subjects. At the time, I didn't realize how important those classes were to my overall development as a person. I am especially grateful that eighth grade girls were required to take home economics. I was not at all interested in learning to sew or cook, but after completing my first dress in that class and learning to prepare some simple dishes, I realized how important those life skills are. I am grateful that I learned them in school.

Then it was on to Leilehua High School. Luckily, I had friends from intermediate school so even if we were overwhelmed and felt small compared to the juniors and seniors, we were able to adjust. This was the first time we actually were with students from other grade levels in some of our classes. I was on the college prep track so all of my classes and activities were intended to help me get into college. I had to learn to manage my time to ensure that I got all my work done.

Being involved in extracurricular activities would be important when I applied for college. However at that time, the sports available to girls were pretty limited, and I didn't have any athletic experience. So I got involved in activities like student government, yearbook, and school or class committees. These were extracurricular activities that provided me with positive learning experiences and could be included on my high school resume.

When I look back on my high school years, I have one regret. I wish I had chosen to take some non-college prep courses like music or art even though these were areas where I lacked confidence. Those types of courses could have made me more well rounded, and those experiences would have helped me as an elementary school teacher.

After taking college prep courses like speech, psychology, and note-hand as my electives, however, I was academically prepared to make the transition to college.

As long as I could remember, our parents were volunteering in our community. Dad served as the president of the parent–teacher associations at the public schools we attended. He was on the Mililani Town Association Board and a longtime member of the Lions Club. Dad also coached Little League baseball. Mom was there by his side, supporting him behind the scenes. My parents' volunteerism impacted all of us kids. Every member of our family has given back to our community through coaching youth sports, serving on volunteer boards, and participating in service projects.

Dad wanted to be a high school agriculture teacher, and Mom wanted to be a nurse, but neither was able to go to college to pursue their dreams. Like all parents, though, they wanted their kids to have opportunities that they didn't have, and we understood that our parents would be disappointed if we didn't get a college degree. Mom and Dad never told us what they wanted us to major in when we went to college or what profession to pursue. They allowed us to set our own goals and to be happy with our choices. I know Dad and Mom were proud that we all graduated from college and were successful in our chosen careers: Corinne was the first female attorney general in the state of Hawai'i and retired as the first female Intermediate Court of Appeals judge. Debbie was widowed at a young age, and I will always admire the way she raised her children as a single parent. She presently is the director of governmental affairs and community relations with a development company. Roy held different leadership positions in the private and public sector, and now serves as the managing director for the City and County of Honolulu, and Chris is our Renaissance man. He plays a mean trombone, composes music, and has recorded jazz albums. He could have chosen a career in music, but instead, he is a geneticist and professor in the School of Natural Sciences at the University of California, Merced.

We weren't the only family with success stories. Others from Whitmore Village went on to successful careers in fields such as business, law, education, sports, politics, and medicine. When I look back to our early years, I marvel at how our parents, with limited resources and no real training, were able to instill in all of us a deep desire to learn and to do well in whatever we aspired to. Growing up in our village gave us "roots and wings."

For me, these roots and wings meant that I would spend 45 years as an educator, the last 15 as a principal. It is this journey that forms the basis for this book. ❀

Parenting and Politicking

"We never know the love of a parent till we become
parents ourselves."
—*Henry Ward Beecher*

Parenting

I was already teaching when I met Randy. He was working as a deputy attorney general with my sister Corinne. Our first date was to a University of Hawai'i football game. One date led to another; we attended sporting events, went to movies or walked around Waikīkī, stopping to play Atari games such *Tank* or *Space Invaders* or *Pong*, popular arcade games at the time. Another favorite pastime for Randy was going to look at new cars; he would pick up brochures and speak with salespeople about the features of different models. A little over a year after our first date, Randy and I were married, and about a year later, we became parents. I quickly found out that juggling family and work responsibilities was not easy.

I loved being a wife and mom; somehow, my husband and our sons filled the part of my heart that I didn't know existed. And when each son was born, the size of my heart grew. Each son was special, and I will always wonder how children can have such different personalities when they have the same parents. That was the case with our three sons.

Justin, our firstborn, was an easygoing, pleasant, and observant baby. As an early childhood educator, I knew that talking, playing, singing, and reading to him would prepare him to navigate his world. Justin soaked it all in, and he was an early talker and even learned to read on his own before he was three years old. We would go to the library every week, and come home with a huge bag of books. Justin was always reading, even while having breakfast before leaving for school. That love of learning has always been a trait I've admired in Justin. In fact, he spent an extra semester at the University of Hawai'i taking courses he didn't need since he had more than enough credits to graduate. When I found out and asked him why, he replied that he had his tuition paid via an athletic scholarship and if he didn't take classes he was interested in, he would probably not have that opportunity again. Justin has always loved learning, and now that he is a dad to Jace and Jayden, I see him sharing that love of learning with his boys.

When Jarand came along less than two years later, life changed. Jarand was more feisty and stubborn, and he was determined to do everything his brother was doing. I admit that I underestimated his drive and his abilities; by sheer will, he was able to do things I didn't think he could, like helping us with jigsaw puzzles or playing board games designed for older children. Jarand also enjoyed listening to stories, and when I was busy, the boys would play together or Justin would read books to Jarand. I am sure this is why Jarand learned to read before he started kindergarten. They each had their own bedroom, but most nights, they ended up in the same room, one on the bed, and the other on the floor. The brothers grew up as best friends, a relationship that lasted through their adulthood.

We settled into a comfortable rhythm. Because Randy worked in town and my job was closer to home, I was the designated parent to drop off and pick the kids up at the sitter's or school. Summers were wonderful because the boys and I were able to spend quality time together, going to the library or on spur-of-the-moment field trips or to the park or pool. When Justin and Jarand started playing sports,

I took them to team practices and even volunteered to be a soccer coach, even though I knew very little about the sport. At night, I checked to make sure the boys had completed their homework. We had our share of battles regarding homework, but overall, I loved the life we were building together.

Nearly eight years later, Jordan was born while Randy was still a city councilmember. Being so many years younger than his brothers meant that his life was way less structured than Justin's or Jarand's had been when they were his age. Jordan was dragged around to his brothers' activities, and he was more free-spirited and independent. He didn't want to hold hands when we went walking. He disliked napping. He hated his car seat, and sometimes, I had to stop on the side of the road because he had figured out how to get out and refused to get back in. Jordan was a hands-on learner, and as a sophomore in high school, he built his own computer by researching what he would need, purchasing the parts online, and putting it all together. Jordan was able to graduate with honors from high school, juggling his studies while working part-time at a restaurant. However, he did not enjoy his college experience and ended up dropping out after a few semesters. Unbeknownst to us, Jordan had decided to enlist in the military. His first choice was the Air Force, and he was accepted. We are proud of how he has persevered and become much more independent as a result of his military experiences. Additionally, he is taking advantage of the GI Bill and has resumed taking university courses. He left the Air Force when his commitment ended and is now planning for his future.

Having three sons, all with different personalities, helped me to understand that we need to look at why, how, and what we are teaching so we can engage all students to be curious, to ask questions, and to have the skills to find the answers.

POLITICKING

In 1985 Randy decided to run for political office. A seat had opened on the City Council due to the recall of the previous councilmember for our district. The world I had become comfortable with was suddenly disrupted. I knew that Randy had aspirations of running for political office before we got married, but somehow, the reality of that possibility was difficult for me to grasp. I honestly thought he would wait until the boys were older before deciding to take the plunge. Yet I realized that this was an opportunity that may not come up again, and I knew that Randy was very qualified for the position. After an honest discussion, we were a united team. This meant adjusting my schedule because Randy would be campaigning before and after work, a daunting task for a new candidate who needed to introduce himself to the voting public. We relied on volunteers to do much of the work, and as a family, we did our fair share of what needed to get done, even though Justin and Jarand were only seven and five years old at the time. They learned to stuff envelopes and put on mailing labels and stamps, they held signs with us, and they even canvassed the neighborhood. When Randy won, it was a celebration—not just our family of four, but all our relatives as well as the volunteers who had helped us during the campaign.

As the wife of a politician, life changed. Suddenly, our life wasn't so private anymore. In the first week after Randy was elected to the City Council, parents came up to him at the soccer field to complain that the grass was too tall and hadn't been mowed. Others called him at home at all hours to share concerns; Randy learned to be a good listener. As a rookie councilmember, Randy had opportunities to take positions that impacted our island such as voting against the building of a cannery in Mililani and voting for a moratorium that temporarily stopped new housing projects in Central Oʻahu, directing growth to the "second city" of Kapolei. As a state senator, Randy was instrumental in ensuring that University of Hawaiʻi West Oʻahu would be built in Kapolei rather than Mililani. He believed that the university could be the center around which the "second city" could grow. The decision I believe is most impactful for our City, though, was Randy's opposition to the then mayor's plan to build 1,400 houses in the area known as Waiola in Central Oʻahu. With traffic being a huge concern for the community, Randy opposed the project, but it passed a crucial vote in the City Council. When the project failed to meet the imposed deadlines by the State, Randy met with the community to discuss future use of that area. Randy's vision was for a large 270-acre regional park. Thankfully, then Mayor Harris believed in the project and coordinated a land exchange with Castle & Cooke. Today, that area is known as the Patsy T. Mink Central Oʻahu Regional Park with a world-class tennis complex (recently renamed for our son Jarand M. Y. Iwase); the K. Mark Takai Memorial Aquatic Center; fields for soccer, baseball, softball; walking trails; and an archery center. Every time I go to CORP, I am grateful that Randy had a vision that will keep the area open for future generations.

Our sons grew up much more aware of the issues and the players in local and national politics. Having an attorney–politician dad helped them to see issues from all viewpoints, and they learned how to argue and provide evidence for their opinions. This was important especially when the boys argued with Randy about sports and their favorite teams.

Randy served in elective office for thirteen years until he was appointed to head the Labor Appeals Board. While there, he tackled the backlog of workman's compensation cases and reduced the turnaround time for decision-making. Randy is a stickler for promptness; he shared how some attorneys came in a few minutes after a hearing was scheduled to begin only to find out that the hearing was over. The word got around; attorneys made sure they were early so they wouldn't miss their opportunity to have their client's case heard.

In 2006, Randy ran one last time against a popular incumbent governor. No one wanted to risk their political career to run against her, but Randy believed that the voters deserved a choice. That was probably the most difficult election for me, not only because it was a statewide race which required us to travel to the neighbor islands, but also because I was still learning about the principalship. Additionally, our families at school were experiencing the first of many years of deployments to the Middle East. This was a challenging time, and I felt that I needed to be there for them. Randy lost, and that was his last run for elective office. He decided to retire from public service, and he enjoyed golfing with a buddy, tinkering around the house, reading, following national and local politics, and just relaxing.

After eight years of retired life, Randy was asked by Governor David Ige to chair the Public Utilities Commission. As Hawai'i moves toward a goal of 100 percent renewable energy by 2045, the PUC has an important role in our State. Randy served during the governor's first term, and decided to retire again, this time for good. I think I will always marvel at the variety of jobs Randy has undertaken throughout his professional career: deputy attorney general, city councilmember, Aloha Tower redevelopment director, state senator, Labor Appeals Board chairperson, and Public Utilities Commission chairperson. All of these positions were in public service, requiring vastly different skill sets. Throughout his career, Randy has impacted the future of our State by helping to shape policies. I am proud of all he has accomplished.

I look back and I realize that no matter how hectic life was especially with Randy involved in politicking, I enjoyed those days. Being able to juggle everything really made me a more efficient person. I learned to prioritize, and despite all of the responsibilities, our family always came first. I have warm memories of those days when our boys were growing up, and I hope they recall those days with fondness as well. I also believe that having to prioritize my life as well as being more aware of the issues that are important to our State and the nation helped me greatly when I became a principal. ❀

My Life as a Teacher

"A teacher affects eternity. He can never tell where his influence stops."
—*Henry Adams*

Why did I become a teacher? I've been asked that question many times in my life. I decided that I wanted to be a teacher in kindergarten, and for some reason, I never changed my mind. I liked the idea of being in charge of a classroom of students, helping them to learn something new.

When I was growing up, "teacher" was an acceptable profession for females. Teacher, nurse, or secretary—those were traditionally female positions. We didn't grow up in a time of gender equity or Title IX, and few women went to medical or law school as they do today. My older sister, Corinne, was one of the exceptions; after participating on the debate team in high school, she aspired to be an attorney. At the time, there was no law school here in Hawai'i, so she applied to and was accepted to Baylor Law School and had a successful career.

I had already decided when I entered the University of Hawai'i that I wanted to be a teacher, preferably with younger children. It was my dream to give students a positive beginning and a love for learning they would take with them throughout their years in school. I was accepted to the College of Education prior to my junior year. It was the perfect time because the university was just starting a new Early Childhood Education program where essential skills were addressed through a hands-on, multi-disciplinary approach. Our lessons were integrated and student-centered, and during my student teaching experience at the University Lab School, I was able to try some of these lessons with the kindergarten and first graders I worked with. Seeing the kids' excitement and engagement convinced me that this strategy would be useful when I had my own classroom.

I was student teaching and in my final semester in 1973 when teachers in the Department of Education went on strike. The resulting pay raise that teachers received meant that there was a significant reduction in force, and the three-on-two program in elementary schools (three teachers for two classrooms of students) was disbanded. This was clearly not a good time to be looking for a job as an elementary school teacher. Fortunately, I was able to secure a job with Head Start, a program that was created in 1965 as part of President Johnson's War on Poverty. I was grateful for this opportunity; many of my classmates were unable to secure teaching positions, and we lost some good teachers as a result.

HEAD START

I was so excited to finally have my own classroom! I set up my room, went on home visits to meet the students and their parents, and started to plan for the first days of school. Truthfully, though, I had never set up a classroom or started off the school year because I student-taught during the spring semester when the setup and routines were already established. I thought the room looked inviting and perfect, but after the first day of school, I realized I needed to make changes to the room arrangement because we can't expect three- and four-year-olds not to touch when they see something that interests or intrigues them. I needed to safety-proof the classroom while also having teaching materials and activities that students can touch. In all the years that I taught—not just with Head Start—I was always moving things around, changing activities on the shelves, and bringing in artifacts or creatures for us to learn about together.

Working with economically disadvantaged preschool students validated my core education beliefs about equity, learning through play, collaborating as a team, the importance of parent involvement and engagement, and early interventions. More than that, though, I got to see the results firsthand, when these students, who were considered at-risk, had quality educational services that address the whole child. Head Start provided health services, free meals, social services, and parent education in addition to addressing the needs of every child to prepare them to be successful in kindergarten and beyond.

Many of the students entered Head Start with deficits in their overall development especially in oral and receptive language. Most of our students had never held a book in their hands or listened to a story until they started school. By the end of the year, they loved story time and were raising their hands to answer questions. They were also borrowing books to read at home with their parents. This was critical because language is essential to the development of literacy skills when students begin their formal school experience. As an early childhood advocate, I believe that play is a child's work and that we can learn much about children's strengths and needs by observing them as they play, either individually or with others. Our quarterly progress assessments and team meetings helped me as a teacher to ensure that our classroom environment provided opportunities for students to grow and develop to their fullest potential to make up for any deficits when they entered our program.

Parents were an integral part of the Head Start program. We encouraged and trained them to help out in the classroom, working with individuals or small groups of students. Student needs were addressed in a more timely manner with the extra bodies in the classroom. Some of our parents volunteered daily, and by the end of the year, they were comfortable leading the whole group in a read-aloud or other similar activity. I am proud that many of these parent volunteers applied for and were hired as educational assistants, and some even went on to get their credential to become teachers, thereby breaking the poverty cycle that may have held them back. I feel strongly that connections with our parents benefit the students and staff at a school, and I wish that more teachers had the opportunity to see the value in training parents as volunteers in the classroom.

Another requirement of Head Start is that 10 percent of the students have identified special needs with an Individualized Education Program to address any developmental delays. These students were mainstreamed in the general education setting with push-in or pull-out resource services. Working with these students and learning different strategies to help them progress made me realize the importance of inclusive classroom environments where students with special needs are in the same classroom with normally developing students. In my fifteen years with the program, I learned so much from our special needs students. The most important lesson was that all students can learn, no matter what challenges they may face.

I was fortunate to start my career as an educator at Head Start. When I reflect on my beginning as a teacher, I realize how much I had to learn on the job, and I am grateful for my supervisors who provided the support I needed to grow and who encouraged me to try new ideas. I gained valuable experiences that made me a better teacher.

HAWAI'I DEPARTMENT OF EDUCATION

I loved teaching Head Start, but it was always my hope to be able to teach in a public elementary school. After fifteen years, I finally received an opportunity with the Hawai'i State Department of Education as a preschool special education teacher at Wheeler Elementary School. Although I was not SPED-certified, I took the job to get my foot in the door. This was my first time in an actual elementary school where I was part of a department. There were 12 students in our classroom with a variety of needs ranging from speech delays to those diagnosed with autism. My previous experience at Head Start prepared me well for this position. We focused on social and academic skills but also addressed the students' individual needs in their Individualized Education Program. I strongly believe in early intervention; these three- and four-year-olds made such progress during their year in that classroom. In fact, several of the students were able to enter kindergarten with limited special education services after a year in our classroom.

After that year, I was assigned to a second grade general education position at Wheeler Elementary. The school was on base and serviced Air Force and Army dependents as well as some local students who lived off base in the school's geographical area. This was my first time teaching on a grade level, and our team was a mix of experienced as well as probationary teachers. It was wonderful to be part of a grade level that supported each other, and we were encouraged by our principal to try new ideas. We shared strategies to engage our students through integrated thematic units as well as author studies. As a teacher with a range of learners and learning styles, I used a variety of strategies to personalize learning for students and to help them become more responsible for their own learning. I was fortunate to be selected to attend a series of professional development sessions on math problem solving, and it changed how I taught math. I saw the value in collaborative group work and student discussions about different ways to solve the same problem. It was refreshing to see students conversing about math problems, and I noticed that these discussions reinforced their understanding of number concepts.

In 1993, a brand-new "high-tech" school was opening up, the first of its kind in our state, and I applied to teach there. I was fortunate and excited to be selected as one of the first teachers at Mililani Mauka Elementary School. The expectations were high, but all of the staff worked together to ensure that our students would be provided with a first-class education. I was in a first–second grade loop—we taught the same students for two years—and we implemented interdisciplinary units that focused on deeper learning. We had four student computers—a far cry from today's one-to-one classrooms—but at the time, this was a high-tech environment. I definitely was not a techie back then, but I learned different ways that technology could be used to engage students and personalize instruction for first and second graders.

Working at Mililani Mauka showed me that when students enter kindergarten with positive preschool experiences, when parents are fully engaged in ensuring that their children are in school and ready to learn, and when the expectations for learning have no ceiling, students will thrive. I was constantly amazed at my students' growth from the time they entered as eager first graders until they left our classroom, ready for the rigors of third grade.

I loved being a teacher; every day was an adventure, and creating positive relationships within our classroom was so rewarding. We were a family, helping each other to grow and develop to our fullest potential. Relationships were so important, and it warmed my heart to see kids helping each other without being asked. Of course I had my share of challenging students, but I never gave up on a child. This was especially true when I looped with my students at Mililani Mauka. Knowing that they would be in our classroom for two years strengthened my drive to create strong personal relationships with the students and their families. I believe that looping has so many benefits, and I wish more teachers would be open to trying it.

For me, teaching was not just a job. I loved the students' curiosity and their enthusiasm for learning. I enjoyed learning new ideas and seeing trends in education based on research. I believe that I improved my craft with each class and each student I was privileged to teach. I truly felt that I was so lucky to be doing something I really loved.

One day, my principal asked me a question, "Have you ever

thought about going into administration?" The question caught me by surprise, and I answered honestly that I never had. "Think about it," she suggested. I attended a meeting for those interested in going into administration and had an opportunity to speak with principals and ask questions. I discussed it with Randy and when he decided to leave politics and take an appointment to be the chair of the Labor Appeals Board, the timing seemed right. And that started the next chapter in my journey as an educator. ✤

My Life as a Principal

"If your actions inspire others to dream more, learn more,
do more, and become more, you are a leader."
—*John Quincy Adams*

Becoming a Principal

When I was a student, all of my principals were male. I didn't even know what a principal did every day; the only thing I heard was that they could paddle students who misbehaved. I saw my principals around the school usually wearing a shirt and tie, but I never engaged in conversations with them. Somehow, the word "principal" equated to being in trouble, and I wouldn't have wanted that.

I realized the importance of a strong school leader when I became a teacher. My supervisors at Head Start and my principals in the Hawai'i State Department of Education were supportive and really helped me to grow professionally to become a better educator. I was fortunate because I was never micromanaged, and that gave me the courage to try new ideas and to expand my thinking beyond our classroom and our school. So when I became a principal, my goal was to be someone who would provide the support for our teaching staff to continuously improve, which in turn, would positively impact our students. I believed that relationship building would create the kind of supportive and trusting environment where teachers and students could flourish, not just in the class-room or in school, but in life.

As we were going through our program to become school administrators, we were told that due to upcoming retirements, we might be selected for a principalship pretty quickly. Therefore, as a vice principal, I learned as much as I could about the Department of Education and its policies. I was able to view the school from a different perspective. No longer was I one among many teachers, I was now one of two administrators. I asked lots of questions, discussed issues with my principal, and gained experience in leading and supporting our staff. After 2.5 years, I applied for and was selected to be the principal at Hale Kula Elementary School.

Hale Kula Elementary School was located on the Schofield Barracks Army installation. With the construction of new housing units from 1955 to 1962, to accommodate returning soldiers of the 25th Infantry Division and their families, there was a need for an elementary school, and Hale Kula opened in 1959, the same year that Hawai'i became a state. Our families came from many different states and countries. Being stationed in Hawai'i was an opportunity for our students and their families to experience our diverse cultures and to learn our unique history. Living in Hawai'i also has its challenges, such as being away from the support of extended family, having to make new friends, and unfamiliarity with our local culture.

CHALLENGES

When I began, we had fewer than 500 students, due to the privatization of housing on Schofield. Homes in our area were razed to make room for newer models. As the privatized homes were completed, enrollment at our school began to increase at an alarming rate, and by 2012 we were overcrowded with more than 1,000 students. Every room at the school was being used, and we even built a dividing wall in several of our portable classrooms to accommodate all of our students and staff. As a school, we needed to be creative and work together to address these kinds of problems so that teaching and learning would be minimally impacted.

In 2004, troops from Schofield began deploying to the Middle East. Many families experienced multiple year-long deployments until about 2012, when the last units returned home. Deployments were stressful, and as a school, we needed to address the emotional challenges our students and families were facing. Having a parent or a spouse in harm's way was stressful; we noticed students who did not want to come to school, preferring to stay at home with the remaining parent. Other students refused to talk about their fears, but it was evident that something was bothering them. That's when our partnership with the Tripler Army Medical Center School Mental Health Team blossomed. A TAMC psychiatrist, psychologist, and social worker works with the school team to address the needs of students who are struggling educationally due to physiological or mental health issues. Having offices on our campus provides convenience for families and allows these medical professionals to observe students in the classroom and to collaborate with the school team to come up with a plan of action that we could all agree to implement.

A primarily military-impacted school faces challenges that are unique to the families they serve. It is not unusual for students to attend several different schools in one academic year until they move into their "permanent" housing while in Hawai'i. A majority of the students are able to handle these transitions; they are resilient and academically, they are able to adjust. There are other students, however, who have great difficulty with these transitions, and they may require social, emotional, and/or academic supports. Our staff takes these challenges in stride. Often, teachers will review their roster at the end of the year and realize that less than half of their students were in their class for the full school year. We were fortunate to have staff who were committed to our clientele. Many of them started and ended their career at our school. We also hired military spouses who were in Hawai'i for a few years; they understood the challenges of teaching in a military-impacted school, and they were able to relate to the families we served.

Prioritizing Job Responsibilities

Being organized and being able to prioritize is essential in the principalship. I never knew what would happen through the course of the day so it was best to be prepared. Some days were calm and I could do what I enjoyed best: visit classrooms and listen to students share what they were learning. Other days were back-to-back meetings or one "crisis" after another. There were many days when I'd look at the clock and realize that I had forgotten to eat lunch or that it was already time to go home.

I started the day early, and the first task was to check my e-mail while I was still at home. It's amazing the amount of e-mails a principal receives. I got to school early, and oftentimes, our clerk was already there, making phone calls to secure substitutes while I tried to problem-solve in case we couldn't find anyone. Despite the fact that we had an automated system, finding substitutes was an ongoing challenge. Getting an early start to the day enabled me to assist with last-minute schedule changes and also provided me time to meet with staff through drop-in or planned conversations or meetings. I found that scheduled morning meetings were a preferred option for many teachers, and sometimes, the best time for staff members to drop by was when they were signing in at the counter right outside the principal's office.

As much as possible, I liked to be out in the mornings to greet the students and families. Sometimes it meant opening car doors in the drop-off line. Other times, it meant walking around the school and talking to students in the waiting area. And occasionally, I did crossing guard duty when the military volunteers were absent. There is an optimistic cheeriness in the morning, and even those who experienced challenges the day before knew that a new day brought opportunities to turn things around.

At school, I always had my lanyard with a bunch of keys around my neck and a small handbag that I wore over my shoulder. In that bag was a walkie-talkie and my trusty iPhone. The walkie-talkie was invaluable for communicating with the custodians or the office. During the school day, I primarily used my phone to document what was going on at our school. Teachers were proud when I took photos of their classroom, their students, or student work because they knew I would share them in the staff bulletin or on our school Facebook or Twitter page. This was also a great way for our school community to be informed about the great things happening in our classrooms.

My favorite part of the job was seeing students excited about what they were learning. It also became my habit to check in on certain students regularly. Developing a positive relationship with our most challenging students supported not only the student but the teacher as well. There were days when I could hear a teacher's sigh of relief when I walked through the door.

Supporting Our Staff and Students

Supporting our staff was a priority for me. Our carefully crafted budget put student learning first; this meant providing the personnel and the funds to ensure that our students would have a well-rounded education as well as the resources to thrive. Supporting our staff also meant creating opportunities for the conversations that would help teachers reflect and set goals for themselves. Our instructional coaches worked individually as well as with grade levels to review and analyze data and to set goals for students. They also worked with grade level teachers to address benchmarks for all core subject areas. Coaching and mentoring was essential for new teachers, and grade level or department colleagues as well as a designated mentor provided that support. Teachers worked for the entire school year within a professional learning community on an area they wanted to explore and learn more about; this became part of their self-reflection that is so essential for self-improvement.

As a principal, meetings took up a good portion of the week—meetings for students, meetings with staff, meetings with other principals, meetings with the community, meetings with parents. Meetings are a part of the job, and I had an open-door policy so despite those hectic days, when someone came to the door and asked, "Are you busy? I want to share something with you," I made time to listen to them. I realize that these small conversations went a long way to building a trusting and open relationship with our staff and a school culture that created opportunities for everyone at our school to contribute to our continued growth as individuals and as a community.

Then there were the crises that needed immediate attention. An upset student leaving the classroom triggered a "Code Nike," and all available adults with walkie-talkies would search for the child until we were sure that he or she was safe. Or it could be a physical altercation between students, or a parent demanding to see the principal, or anything else requiring me to drop what I was doing and tend to the situation. Fortunately, these crises did not happen regularly. I learned to be a good listener. I realized that when someone is upset—a student, staff member, or parent—listening to their concerns and asking clarifying questions before responding usually defused the situation. It also helped to follow up and get back to the person in a timely manner. By then, the situation had usually worked itself out.

In 2013, based on a facilities assessment of all schools located on military bases in the United States, Hale Kula Elementary School received a $33.2 million Congressional and State allocation to address the condition and capacity of our school. After three years of living with dust, noise, and general inconveniences, the project was completed, and the result was amazing! All classrooms were renovated, and we now have four new state-of-the-art buildings—an administration building, a ten-classroom building, a library/

media/student center, and a covered play court. On April 19, 2016, just as the project was nearing completion, the Board of Education approved the renaming of our school from Hale Kula Elementary School to Daniel K. Inouye Elementary School. Senator Inouye was a staunch advocate for education and for military children, so this was a fitting tribute.

As I look back at my schedule as a principal, the day began in the early morning, usually before 5 a.m. when I read and responded to any e-mails or messages that came in during the previous night or early morning. It ended in the evening when I caught up on whatever I couldn't get to during the day. It was also a great time to catch up on social media and to do some professional learning via my personal learning network. It was a routine that worked for me, and until I retired, I didn't realize how much this schedule dictated my life. ✤

PART TWO

MY CORE VALUES AND BELIEFS

"When your values are clear to you,
making decisions becomes easier."
—*Roy E. Disney*

.

LEADING WITH ALOHA

"Our core beliefs are at the very center of who we are,
what we believe about ourselves, what we think of others,
and how we feel about life as a whole."
—*Alethia Luna*

By the time I became a principal, my core values and beliefs were strongly embedded in who I was as a person, as an educator, and as a leader. My life, growing up in a rural pineapple plantation community, was simple but fulfilling. I loved learning in school, which made me want to become a teacher. When I achieved my dream to become an educator, I realized that all my university experiences didn't quite prepare me for the realities of what a teacher does every day, but I was willing to learn. Becoming a wife and a mom added to who I was and how I related to others which in turn, further ingrained the essential values and beliefs which I live by. All of my experiences—my successes as well as my challenges—made me much more aware of the importance in building positive relationships with others, and that is what I believe was most important for me as a leader.

Everyone is different. Every child, every adult. I saw that in my own children and in my students and staff. Our life experiences help to shape who we are, what we expect of ourselves, and how we treat others. As educators, we hold the future of our students in our hands, and supporting them to be their best is a huge responsibility.

The principal plays a major role in how the school is perceived by the community. I chose to lead our school with aloha. This meant treating others with love, compassion, empathy, and respect, being open to listening when there was a concern, being visible around campus, disciplining in private, and welcoming new students and families to become a part of our ʻohana (family). It also meant celebrating and sharing our successes with our school community. The principal takes the lead in how people treat each other. If the principal models aloha, teachers will treat their students with aloha, and students will treat each other similarly. The principal models that expectation.

As a school leader, personally connecting with our school community was essential. It is not easy at a military-impacted school where students are constantly transitioning in and out throughout the year. One of the challenges at our military-impacted school was overcoming the negative perception of Hawaiʻi schools. This was a key reason why our school sought accreditation years before the Board of Education made it a requirement for all public schools in Hawaiʻi, and we never regretted our decision to go through the rigorous self-study process. We also welcomed parents to volunteer at the school, shared what was going on in the classrooms via social media, and hosted family events that encouraged parent–child participation.

Creating a positive relationship with our staff was also important. I made it a priority to get to know each one personally as well as professionally. We laughed together, and I was the shoulder they could cry on. We celebrated life and we mourned the passing of a life. We were a family, and our staff needed to know that we would support them when times were great as well as when times got tough. I wanted teachers to feel comfortable when I popped into their classrooms and to know that when I took photos, it was a good thing, not a "gotcha." When they saw me interacting with students or listening in on the lesson, they relaxed. These classroom visits became starters for professional conversations with teachers. I found that often, the best professional discussions were the result of a pop-in visit to the classroom as opposed to a formal observation.

As a principal, I made many decisions each day. Some were made at the spur of the moment while others were made after seeking feedback from our school community. The relationships I nurtured as well as my core values and beliefs about leadership and learning helped to guide me in my decision-making. As a school leader, I made decisions based on what is best for students or for that individual student. I trusted our staff and school community to be innovative and to try new ideas to support our students. I believe in the value of teamwork because one person alone cannot accomplish what a team of people can. I believe that everyone has strengths and can contribute positively to our school community. I believe in the power of coaching, self-reflection, and goal-setting as essential to self-improvement, and I know that as a principal, continuous improvement meant continuously learning. These were the core values and beliefs that formed the basis of the decisions I made as a principal. I chose to lead with aloha because I believe that we all had the same goal: to ensure that our students are happy and successful, not just in school, but in the life they will lead after they leave us. ✤

BE AN ADVOCATE FOR STUDENTS

"I believe the children are our future,
Teach them well and let them lead the way.
Show them all the beauty they possess inside."
—*"Greatest Love of All,"*
Linda Creed and Michael Masser, songwriters

During my first semester as a principal, I had to make a difficult decision. Our enrollment had declined, and I carefully examined our school budget. I realized that we no longer had the resources to support our reading program, which required extra personnel and an expectation that we would monitor teachers to ensure they were following the program with fidelity. Making a decision so soon after taking over as principal was unexpected, and some members of our school community asked me to reconsider. I refused; I knew that in the long run, our students would benefit when teachers were empowered to try different strategies and to use different resources. Grade level teachers began collaborating and sharing ideas about what worked for them or with specific students. They worked together to create interdisciplinary units that paired science or social studies standards with language arts and other content standards. They created common assessments and reviewed data to ensure that their students were on target to achieve grade level standards. They were trusted to do what was best for their students, and the results were evident in the classrooms where teaching and learning became more engaging and relevant. To this day, I believe that making that decision and doing what was right for students was a make-or-break moment for my principalship. Our teachers' trust in my leadership and the community's trust in our school were strengthened.

Principals have many responsibilities at their school. They ensure that the school's vision and mission are implemented. Principals oversee the curriculum; monitor student achievement; encourage parent and community involvement; implement department, district, or school policies and procedures; create a financial plan and oversee the budget; hire and evaluate staff; and ensure the safety and upkeep of the facilities. If I were to consolidate all of a principal's roles into one statement, it would be this. Principals are advocates for their students. Everything we do comes back to the question, "How will this support our students?"

Transition Supports

Everyone contributes to the success of a school, but every school is different. Our school needed to address the transient lifestyle of our military families, and first impressions were so important. We were one of the first elementary schools in the state to establish a Transition Center with a transition coordinator and a student Greeters Club, a place where our new students and families could receive a tour of our school, ask questions, and be welcomed to be a part of our 'ohana. Our whole school community worked together to make families feel like a part of our school from their first day to their last. Our custodial staff kept our campus clean and safe and when a teacher asked for another desk for the new student who would be entering her class the next day, they responded immediately. Our cafeteria staff prepared nutritious breakfasts and lunches because they knew that when children are hungry, learning may be impacted. Our office staff greeted our new students and families warmly, answering questions patiently and making sure all the registration forms were completed so the child could start school. Our teachers understood the challenges our military-impacted students face, and they welcomed them into their classroom, making sure the child learned classroom and school routines and made new friends. Our support staff was there to help students who might need interventions, counseling services, or specialized services to be successful in school. Due to the military lifestyle of moving a family every few years, there were some students who fell through the cracks and were struggling academically. We were there to provide supports for them. Everyone was there for the students.

Student-centered Decision-making

When I became the principal of our school, one of my first tasks was reviewing our students' standardized test scores. I knew that the scores would be published in the local paper and that the public often judged schools by their test scores. I thought that test scores were a reflection of me as a principal and that our school community would compare us to other schools with better results. I quickly realized that this was the wrong focus; we want students to do their best on standardized tests, but a student is much more than a test score.

Based on discussions with our staff, we refocused our energies from test scores to providing our students with a well-rounded education that included the arts and physical education. We sought grants to upgrade our computers so our students had opportunities to use these devices to enhance learning. We chose to transition to project-based learning where students were actively involved in real-world problems such as the impact of trash in the oceans, raising awareness about accepting and including everyone, creating resources for our Schofield families to become familiar with their community, or examining how we can all make a difference by reducing waste. Students then shared with an authentic audience about how they were making a difference in their school or community. What we discovered was that even students who struggled with academics were invested in their own learning when they realized that they could contribute their ideas and participate in sharing what they had learned.

COMMITMENT TO STUDENTS

Educators believe in doing their best for today's children so they can positively contribute to their world and their future. It takes special people to commit themselves to preparing our next generation for a life that is constantly and continuously evolving. Teachers have special skills, learned in their university coursework and on the job, but skills and knowledge are not enough. The most effective teachers I had the privilege to work with had the heart that is so essential when one works with our young people. They realize that teaching is not easy; it takes time, discipline, patience, resilience, and a true commitment to be the best they can be for the sake of their students.

Like their students, no two teachers are alike, and past experiences influence how they interact with students. We were fortunate to have wonderful teachers at our school who really put students first: caring teachers who stayed after school, helping struggling students so they could be successful in their learning; firm teachers who made sure students knew that they expected the best from them, behaviorally and academically; creative teachers who learned and used innovative practices in the classroom to engage students; compassionate teachers who brought personal care items or school supplies for those students who did not have any. Our teachers taught with aloha.

Educators strive to engage and empower students so they can be their best, to overcome any challenges, and to realize that they are an integral member of our community. We encourage open communication with parents because they are essential to the success of their children. We help students to self-reflect when their behavior is unacceptable, to take responsibility for their own actions, and to learn from their mistakes so it doesn't happen again. We address the whole child because students have different strengths and challenges that make them unique individuals. We provide interventions or additional services if students need a higher level of support. Our goal is always to advocate for our students so they can experience success.

PRIORITIZING SPENDING

At a school, the principal is ultimately responsible for making spending decisions. Although the State can recommend what resources to use or purchase, the school needs to determine priorities based on the needs of their students. This was always a challenge because there never was enough funding to cover everything we wanted to provide. At our school, focusing on what's best for our kids made decision-making easier. That meant allowing teachers flexibility in the resources they used to teach grade level curriculum, making staffing decisions that ensured our students a well-rounded education and the supports they needed for success in school and in life, and seeking grants or other funding sources so our students could benefit. It meant updating technology devices but also making sure that those devices were used by students to explore, discover, create, and share and not just for drills or as a substitute textbook. It meant providing our staff with professional development opportunities as well as time to collaborate with their colleagues so they could learn with and from each other. Teachers had wish lists of things they wanted to purchase if extra funds were available. Again, determining priorities based on student need made purchasing decisions easier.

I look back at the child I was when I started kindergarten all those years ago. I had no idea about the world that would open for me once I started school. I wanted our students to experience the wonder of learning, of making friends and working with others, of having the confidence to try something new, and about learning from their mistakes and their peers. I wanted them to dream dreams and to realize that school was a great place for learning. As an educator, I was an advocate for our students.

Leading with aloha meant:

• Making the kinds of meaningful changes necessary so that teaching and learning is relevant

• Getting to know students and staff as individuals because "one size fits all" doesn't work if we truly believe in supporting all children

• Carefully crafting a budget that emphasizes supports for students and educating the whole child

• Supporting our staff so they can, in turn, provide enriching learning opportunities for students

• Being an advocate for students ❋

Be Open to New Ideas

"What good is an idea if it remains an idea? Try. Experiment.
Iterate. Fail. Try again. Change the world."

—*Simon Sinek*

When I attended school, I never thought of myself as a creative person. I struggled with art, and although I enjoyed music, I had no musical talent. I felt uncomfortable during activities that required creativity and rarely contributed to discussions. I was always looking for the "right" answer, and that's not what creativity is.

I was determined to change that for my students when I became a teacher. Knowing that play is important for the development of young minds, my students had opportunities to interact with building or art materials and to participate in creative movement, dramatic play, and open-ended writing activities. Young students are naturally creative, and I wanted them to have the confidence that I lacked, both as a student and as an adult.

As a teacher, I was constantly looking to improve my lessons to provide opportunities for students to be creative and to share their ideas. I observed that my young students were not inhibited. They readily participated in brainstorming sessions where all responses were accepted, and often, students presented ideas that I would never have thought of. I also learned much by observing other teachers, asking questions, reading professional literature, attending workshops or conferences, and continuing to grow as a teacher. It was important for me to know that I could improve what I was doing so I could be my best for my students.

As educators, it is important to be open and to share new ideas and effective ways of teaching and learning. Our profession is changing rapidly with innovative technology, research on the brain and how we learn, and a world that is changing so quickly that what our students learn today may be outdated by the time they graduate. Today's students are different, too. They have ready access to information so our assignments need to be more relevant if we want to engage them in their learning.

TRUSTING OUR TEACHERS

When I first became a principal, I wanted our teachers to know that I trusted them to be innovative in their teaching practices. Previously, they had been monitored to ensure that they were following the school-wide reading program with fidelity, and teachers probably thought I would continue that practice. Discontinuing the reading program in the first months of my principalship gave me a unique opportunity to show our teachers that my leadership style was not to micromanage; I trusted them to do what was best for their students. My goal as principal was to encourage our teachers to teach students, to get to know them—their interests, their strengths, their challenges—and to adjust their instruction so their students could be successful. Teachers began talking with each other, sharing lessons, and trying new ideas. I think they were excited to be trusted to do what they had gone to college for: to teach students.

After that, our teachers were comfortable about trying new strategies or using different resources to teach. They also experimented with new technology tools in their classrooms. Although our teachers were addressing the same grade level standards, they were empowered to use teaching strategies and resources that worked for them and their students. Our teachers' enthusiasm and their commitment to try new ways of teaching had a positive impact on our students, not just academically, but socially and behaviorally as well. I believe that when teachers are excited about innovating or trying new methods to address content standards, their students benefit. Additionally, new teachers to our school were able to share what they had used in their previous experiences. We learned from them, and they learned from us.

HOPE GARDEN

One idea was proposed by a general education teacher and a special education teacher who would be co-teaching in a classroom. They asked to dig up the whole area in front of their classroom wing to create a garden. The teachers saw this as an opportunity to address grade level language arts, math, science, and social studies standards through hands-on learning. Their enthusiasm was contagious, and after several discussions, I realized that this was a terrific opportunity, not just for these teachers and their students, but for the whole school. The students named their labor of love "Hope Garden," and they were invested in their garden and in their learning. They came in on their breaks or stayed after school to harvest vegetables or to weed and clean up the area to make room for the next planting. They led visitors on tours of their garden and explained about vermiculture or composting or why they surrounded their vegetable plants with marigolds or how insects help with pollination. Students couldn't wait to cook and taste their vegetables and to market their harvest. Today, new teachers and students have taken over and continue to expand the lessons learned over time. We see evidence of how a garden can provide unlimited real-world learning opportunities for a lifetime.

VIRTUAL SCHOOL COMMUNITY MEETING

A school is more than the staff, so we also solicited ideas from our parents and our students. We believed that everyone could contribute innovative ideas when given the opportunity.

One of our innovative ideas came from a parent. For years since Act 51 was passed by the Legislature in 2004, we invited our parents to participate in our twice-a-year School Community meetings where we could share our school's progress as well as ask for input for our academic and financial plans. We tried different ideas to engage our families including offering babysitting services, holding the meetings during different times of the day or evening, pairing these meetings with student performances, and offering door prizes. Nothing worked; participation was minimal. At a School Community Council meeting, a parent representative suggested a virtual meeting via Facebook. We decided to give it a try. Setting up the meeting was relatively easy, and by crafting open-ended questions, sharing positive behavioral expectations, and giving parents and staff opportunities to share concerns as well as suggestions, participation in our School Community meetings rose significantly. Our military-impacted parents as well as our staff appreciated that they could join in on the meeting wherever they were, as long as they had internet connection. We even had soldier–parents who were temporarily off-island make the time to engage in the discussions. This idea, proposed by a parent, greatly increased participation and engagement by the community in our mandatory meetings.

STUDENT VOICE

Even kids had the opportunity to share their ideas. Our construction project was nearing completion, and we would regain our playgrounds for recess use. How could we redesign our recess areas to maximize teaching and learning opportunities for students? Students loved being asked for their ideas, and they enthusiastically researched ideas on the computer. Although some of their plans were grandiose and unfeasible, we listened and incorporated some of their ideas into our recess procedures. For example, students felt that recess was too short so we lengthened the time on Wednesdays when we had only one scheduled recess due to our earlier release time for teacher meetings. Students shared that recess was an opportunity to be less structured and to play with others who were not in their classroom so we let students dig in the dirt, run around the trees, and make up their own games. Students felt that too many rules and consequences made recess less fun, and it was hard for adults to adjust at first because safety was always our primary concern. Eventually, though, we realized that recess was a perfect time for students to make up their own games, to settle any disagreements with minimal adult intervention, and to enjoy free play with their peers.

For me, being an effective principal meant listening and encouraging ideas from other members of the school community. It meant trusting others to be innovative, to think of new ways to engage and empower our school community with opportunities they might not have had otherwise. This added to a culture of trust where members of our school community could suggest ideas, knowing we were willing to listen.

Leading with aloha meant:
• Having the confidence to know that great ideas do not come from the principal alone; others in the school community should have a voice in sharing ideas
• Discussing and addressing possible problems or concerns prior to agreeing on a solution
• Monitoring results of our decisions and making changes necessary to continue to move forward
• Nurturing relationships so members feel comfortable about sharing concerns and making suggestions to improve a proposed idea
• Sharing and celebrating our successes and continuing to encourage new ideas and innovative practices ✽

Work as a Team

"Individual commitment to a group effort—that is what makes
a team work, a company work, a society work, a civilization work."
—*Vince Lombardi*

When I was growing up, I didn't understand what it took to be a
part of a team. I didn't play sports or participate in chorus or dance,
and teamwork wasn't really emphasized in school. I believe, however, that it is essential for people to learn to get along and to work together to accomplish a task. In today's world, collaboration can take
place virtually as well as in face-to-face settings, so students need
opportunities to learn to work together towards a common goal.

The Power of Teamwork

It wasn't until I was 16 years old that I learned about the power of
teamwork. It was the summer between my junior and senior year in
high school, and I was going to work for the first time. For most kids
in Hawai'i at that time, we either worked in the pineapple fields or
at the cannery. Since we grew up around pineapple fields in Whitmore, we worked in the fields.

I was assigned to a gang of fifteen females. We had a female *luna*,
or supervisor. Our gang was a mix of experienced, full-time workers
and young first-timers like me. Our first assignment was *hoe hana*,
or weeding. It was so boring, but I think the company wanted to be
sure we could handle eight hours of labor in the hot sun.

After about a week, we received the news we were waiting for. We would actually be picking pineapple! Now we would be doing real work, what we had been hired for! When we got to the field, the luna explained that we would each take a row and would be responsible for picking the pineapples in that row, removing the crown, and putting the fruit onto the conveyor belt, dropping the crown back into the field so it could be picked up later and planted. The old-timers taught us young girls how to twist the crown off. We practiced first with a few pineapples, and then we were assigned to a row. The luna placed each of us newbies between the old-timers.

That first time, there weren't too many pineapples that were ripe enough to pick; only a small percentage were the right color to harvest. That was probably intentional. The company wanted to get us adjusted to the task first before overwhelming us. Even then, though, it was far from easy. Despite all the protective gear—boots, gloves, goggles, canvas chaps, long-sleeved shirt, straw hat—I was getting scratched and poked. My hands were sore from twisting off the crowns, and at times, I was barely keeping up. Luckily, the old-timers were very helpful, even telling us to just drop the whole pineapple onto the conveyor belt, and they would remove the crown. When lunchtime came, I could barely eat my lunch; I just wanted to sit down and rest. Our luna asked us newbies how we were doing, encouraging us to eat our lunch and drink water so we would have energy for the afternoon. I was grateful for her concern.

In time, we were able to keep up with the rest of the gang. There was an incentive for us to work as a team. The company had started a bonus system that combined production and quality of work. It was a complicated formula based on many different factors, and if we exceeded the target for the day, we would get a bonus in our paycheck at the end of the week. Considering that first-year workers were paid $1.40 per hour, the promise of a bonus motivated all of our gang to work together to accomplish and exceed the goals. So when a worker was inundated with more pineapples in her row, her neighbors reached over and helped out. When a bin was filled, especially if we were being pushed extra hard by the driver who set the pace, we sometimes cheered while we waited for the next truck.

When I reflect on my experience as a pineapple field worker, I realize that even though the job itself was challenging, the support from our team was so important. The old-timers wanted us to be successful, and they did what they could to help us develop the skills we needed to be an effective member of the team. Those ladies taught me about unselfishness and working together to achieve a goal. They helped us to improve so that we could contribute to the team.

Teamwork in the Classroom

As a teacher, I applied what I learned about teamwork as I planned lessons in my classroom. I deliberately prepared team-building activities so students would recognize that everyone has something to contribute and that one person alone cannot accomplish what a team of people can. I thoughtfully placed students into mixed ability groups so they could learn to work with others with different strengths as well as individual challenges. As these students grew older, it was my hope that they would take what they learned about working as a team and apply these skills in new situations.

As a principal, I loved dropping into classrooms and observing all of the opportunities students had to collaborate. These included sharing strategies for solving a math problem, working on a shared document or presentation, or using the engineering design process to solve a problem. A culture of collaboration must be established and reinforced in the classroom if we want students to internalize skills that encourage teamwork and take learning to a higher level.

Teamwork at Our School

At our school, students had many opportunities to work on teams as part of their classroom learning experiences. They marketed the vegetables and flowers they grew. They collected school supplies for students in Texas impacted by Hurricane Harvey. They cleared invasive plants on the North Shore and replanted native plants, and they learned more about homelessness and collected personal items for impacted children. Additionally, students learned teamwork through extracurricular activities such as robotics, drama productions, athletic activities, after school enrichment classes, Greeters Club, Junior Police Officers, and student council. Through these kinds of projects and activities, students learned important academic skills as well as non-academic skills such as empathy for others and caring for our community.

Teamwork also applies to the home–school relationship. This was especially important at our school because students and their families were constantly transitioning in or out. Military students face unique challenges, and while moving to Hawai'i can be exciting, it can also add to the stressors which families face. Being so far away from extended family and other systems of support is challenging. Our office staff, transition coordinator, Parent Community Networking Center coordinator, school counselors, and classroom teachers worked together to ensure a smooth transition and adjustment for the students and their families.

We expected our staff to work as a team as well, and I enjoyed seeing experienced and novice teachers working and learning together and helping each other to become better educators. This was evident during grade level or department meetings when teachers shared ideas or examined student work. They agreed to try specific strategies and collect data to gauge student progress. The value of teamwork for teachers is that they can learn from and support each other. Without that support from colleagues, teaching can be a very lonely profession. In fact, one of the reasons why teachers may leave a school or leave teaching altogether is the lack of support and camaraderie that can make a challenging job more manageable.

When our staff works effectively together, our students and school community benefit. Everyone did their part. We depended on our educational assistants to supervise students in the mornings so that everyone got to their classrooms on-time and ready-to-learn. Our cafeteria staff and adult supervisors made suggestions on how to improve procedures for our three lunch periods to minimize traffic congestion and allow adequate time for students to eat. With the number of students enrolling on a daily basis, our office staff worked together to ensure that students could begin as soon as their registration requirements were completed. The military community was essential as well. We met at least once quarterly to share updates and discuss concerns that impacted our schools, and the military provided crossing guards every morning and afternoon so our students could safely cross the streets to get to and from school. Additionally, we were very proud when our custodial team was selected in 2017 as the "Team of the Year" for the Department of Education. They are a perfect example of teamwork, doing whatever is necessary to support our students and teachers while always keeping our campus safe, clean, and inviting.

In today's world, the ability to work as a team is so important. Having the skills necessary to listen and respect other ideas while effectively communicating one's own viewpoint is essential to resolving problems and challenges that face us today and in the future.

Leading with aloha meant:

• Understanding that when we can work together towards a common goal, our school community benefits

• Providing the time and opportunities for all students and teachers to work with others and to develop the collaborative skills necessary to be successful in today's world

• Celebrating the success of teams on our campus

• Providing support so that when teams were experiencing challenges, we could help them overcome their struggles

• Working together—home, school, and community—to address problems that impacted our students. ✿

Everyone Has Strengths

"Here in America, we don't let our differences tear us apart.
Because we know that our greatness comes when we appreciate
each other's strengths, when we learn from each other,
when we lean on each other."

—*Michelle Obama*

Years ago, I did an activity with my second graders. I brought a
bag of apples to class. I asked each student to take one and to ex-
amine it carefully, to notice all the details of that apple. After a few
minutes, students shared their observations with their classmates,
and it was amazing that students as young as seven years old could
recognize the differences in each apple. We discussed the implica-
tions of their observations, and I think their reflections are applica-
ble to our work in schools. For example: Each apple may look the
same, but upon examining their apple closer, students noticed the
details that made their apple different. *We may look similar but everyone has individual personalities and character traits.* Each apple may
have had a slight imperfection—a brown spot, a little dot, etc.—but
the rest was just fine. *No one is perfect. It's the imperfections that make
us special.* What we observed was just the outside. We don't know
what the apple was like on the inside. *Our job as educators is to get to
know others on the inside, not just the outside. Only then can we really
help that person gain the most from their experience in our classroom
or at our school.* Sometimes, students needed reminders about listening to what their classmates were saying. *Listening to others helps*

to broaden our viewpoints and can help to build understanding and
tolerance for others.

STUDENT STRENGTHS AND CHALLENGES

In my 45 years as an educator, I worked with thousands of children and hundreds of teachers. They all had strengths, and they had challenges as well. The key is to find their strengths and build on them so that the challenges become less significant. This is especially important for students who are English language learners (those whose native language is not English), those identified with special education services, or students who have social or emotional challenges or who have negative attitudes towards school.

A military community is diverse, and we had students who spoke little or no English, some from countries I couldn't even pronounce. Being a new kid in the class in the middle of the year is already difficult; imagine not speaking any or very little English as well. One trait these students possessed was resilience; they may have been frustrated, but they didn't give up. They were great at observing their classmates, and they did well in classes like art and physical education where they could watch what others were doing and follow along. Our ELL staff and classroom teachers worked with these students using multiple strategies and resources so they could begin to pick up the language. It is amazing how quickly some students progressed in their understanding of the English language and became proficient enough to require minimal services later on. I have great admiration for these ELL students. They will benefit from being able to speak more than one language.

Our school had a higher-than-average number of students who qualified for special education services (SPED) with an Individualized Education Program (IEP) to address identified concerns. Some had minimal supplementary aids and services whereas others required extensive academic, behavioral, or social supports in order to be successful in the school and classroom setting. Often, transitioning to a new school was more challenging for those with special needs, and there was often a period of adjustment for the child. If necessary, our counselors, behavioral health therapist, and the Tripler School Mental Health Team provided services and worked with the student and family to assist with social or behavioral issues. Through it all, our special education staff got to know these students so they could implement strategies and provide resources to address goals and objectives in their Individualized Education Program. Our staff looked for the student's strengths and interests; they used these as motivators so the child could experience success. Some of those students were knowledgeable about a certain topic; others were wonderful at art or music; some struggled with reading but were whizzes at math; and some students were great athletes. Students with special needs have strengths or interests, and if we focus on what they can do, we may be better able to address their needs.

A FOCUS ON STUDENT STRENGTHS

A positive relationship is key to finding a person's strengths especially for those with significant challenges. All of us are more engaged when what we learn is impactful to us. Studies have shown that when a person has prior knowledge about a subject, learning becomes more meaningful. Finding those interests can engage students and help them understand why they are learning something. We know students with poor literacy skills. When allowed to choose their own book, they are motivated to read and often retain what they've read. We've had students who struggled with reading but when they were able to listen to the book, they retained the information and could participate in discussions. Students who had difficulty writing out an explanation could visually represent their ideas through diagrams or pictures and demonstrate a high level of understanding. When our teachers started their Hope Garden, some of their most enthusiastic and reliable helpers were those students with special needs who volunteered to come in when school was not in session. The teachers were then able to provide the extra academic support in reading, writing, math, or science those students struggled with.

When students in a classroom are aware of the individual strengths of their classmates, group projects can be highly successful in enhancing the learning of everyone. We have seen the outcomes when students' challenges are addressed through the collaborative efforts of the team. When students have options on how to share their learning with others, their confidence grows. We saw kindergarten students who struggled with reading readiness skills lead adults in yoga or teach them how to self-calm when they were feeling stressed. Students who were shy and rarely shared information in class spoke confidently with adult visitors about a project they had completed or a game they had created to share their knowledge about a topic. Additionally, during student-led conferences, all students were able to share work with their parents and to explain what they were proud of and what they could improve. When students are responsible for leading the conference and sharing their strengths and their accomplishments as well as their challenges, the home–school connection is reinforced, and the team can work together to help the child achieve their goals.

A FOCUS ON TEACHER STRENGTHS

Finding teachers' strengths and passions cannot be minimized. Elementary teachers are generalists, meaning they are often expected to teach all subjects. At our school, we hired resource teachers to teach physical education, art, and drama to all students in the school. To provide our students with additional enrichment opportunities, some grade level teachers began teaming to teach subjects such as music, STEM, or health. Our technology team—our librarian, technology coordinator, and technology specialist—were essential resources, assisting students and teachers with finding information and exploring ways to share that information. For example, teachers collaborated with the librarian to plan a series of lessons about simple machines that culminated in students building and sharing simple machines they made using materials available. As part of their social studies standards, students learned about what a community is, designed and named their own community, and collaboratively built it in *Minecraft* with assistance from the technology coordinator. When teachers are enthusiastic and confident about what they are teaching, the students are more likely to be engaged in their learning.

Oftentimes, we don't see the strengths of the child or the teacher because we are so focused on what they cannot do. Let's turn things around and focus on what the child or teacher can do and build on their strengths and interests to address their challenges. In the process, we will build a stronger community of learners in our classrooms and in our schools.

Leading with aloha meant:

• Being aware that everyone is different and that everyone has strengths

• Building on the strengths of students so they can feel confident that they are essential members of their classroom community

• Providing supports for those with more specific needs (e.g. English language learners, students with special needs) so they can be successful now and in their future

• Incorporating the strengths and interests of teachers to positively impact the learning of all students ✤

BE A COACH

"Coaching is unlocking a person's potential to maximize their own performance. It is helping them to learn rather than teaching them."
—Timothy Gallwey

I never thought of myself as a coach. To me, a coach was the one who led athletic teams, the one on the sidelines who made decisions about plays and players. I was a teacher until I volunteered to coach Jarand's soccer team. At that time, soccer was still a fledgling youth sport in Hawai'i, and very few adults had experienced playing the game. The league was desperately looking for coaches, so like a good parent, I volunteered. I figured that I was a teacher and I could handle 15 kids and make sure they had fun at practice and at the games. We lost, 8–0, in our first game. That was humiliating and I felt so badly for our players. We lost again the following week, 4–0, and in our third game, we won, 1–0. We ended up with more wins than losses that season, and I felt that our players improved and enjoyed the game. However, my limited knowledge of soccer impeded my ability to be a truly effective coach, and I knew that in time, what I had to teach the players would not be sufficient to help them improve.

I learned how to be a coach from our son, Jarand. He was 12 years old when he agreed to coach Jordan's soccer team. I spoke with Jarand to make sure he understood the commitment it would take to coach these young five-year-olds. He assured me that he did, and so, although I was the coach on paper, Jarand was the coach at practices and on the field. Even at his young age, Jarand was aware of what it takes to be an effective and respected coach. He saw the strengths as well as areas that each player had to work on. During games, he noticed what the team needed help with, and he planned drills and mini games at practice to address those areas. Coach Jarand decided on a lineup that would take advantage of players' strengths while minimizing their challenges. He needed to know how to put a team on the field that could help each person to grow as a player and as a teammate. Jarand coached for several seasons, and he made competitive soccer fun for his players. He taught soccer skills and strategy, but he also taught about teamwork, perseverance, and sportsmanship. Winning championships was not the main goal for the season; building better players and better people was.

Coaching in the Classroom

After that, in my role as a teacher, I chose to be a coach. It wasn't enough to just teach and hope that students retained what they learned. I wanted students to apply those skills and have opportunities to show us what they had learned. So, instead of completing a worksheet about parts of a letter, my students drafted, edited, and wrote letters to real people, and when they received a response, we were all thrilled! Students learned math concepts through group problem-solving activities where they could discuss different strategies and check the reasonableness of their answers. As a coach, I asked open-ended questions and discovered that students were more responsible for their own learning when they self-reflected and we had honest conversations. Coaching my students changed my whole outlook on how students learn, and I learned to trust them to make the right decisions and to accept responsibility when they failed to make good choices. Coaching was about the students.

Coaching Our Teachers

As a principal, I was responsible to be a supervisor and an evaluator. How I carried out my responsibilities, however, was my choice. I chose to be a coach. If supporting all students was our ultimate responsibility as a school, supporting our teachers and staff was definitely a priority for me as an administrator. Hiring teachers for our school was one of the most challenging tasks I faced as a principal, and supporting their growth was one of the most rewarding. It was our responsibility, as administrators, to provide our teachers with the support and guidance they needed to be successful in their positions and to continue to grow. Our grade level teams and departments, instructional coaches, technology team, and mentor teachers were essential in providing that support. Teaching is a challenging profession but with the right support, all teachers will continue to grow personally and professionally.

The required observations and reflective conversations were opportunities to provide additional coaching support to teachers. Although everyone received the same training and knew what was required for evaluative purposes, the conversations and the actual observation varied depending on the experiences of the teacher. The probing questions during the pre-conference guided teachers to understand that during the observation, I would be looking for evidences of student learning and opportunities for student engagement in the lesson. I felt comfortable in pushing teachers out of their comfort zone, in getting them to understand that taking risks and reflecting on their lessons to make adjustments would help them to grow as teachers and learners. The post-conference was an opportunity for teachers to self-reflect on their lesson and to share any new understandings as a result of the observation experience. Likewise, the other components of the evaluation system provided me with one-on-one time to discuss a teacher's professional goals and growth through the school year. Although these evaluation components were time-consuming, the conversations were invaluable and strengthened my personal and professional connection with our teachers.

As a principal, I went through a period when I felt we needed to collect data on what was going on in classrooms. We spent time as a leadership team creating checklists for walkthroughs. We tried them out, and revised them to get information we thought would be useful when completing our accreditation reports or for required district walkthroughs. We collected data on things like how technology was being used, whether students were collaborating, what the teacher was doing, and whether the learning targets were posted. These checklists didn't work. Teachers felt the information was not accurate and that ten minutes in a classroom didn't really show what students were learning. I agreed with them; I realized that we were taking data for the wrong reasons, to try to quantify what was happening in classrooms when what was really important was the quality of student learning. Rather than checklists, the conversations with students and teachers during and after our walkthroughs were more valuable to inform us about teaching and learning at our school.

Leading as a Coach

Coaches don't play the game; the players do. If a coach is shouting instructions throughout the game, players won't be thinking and making adjustments based on what is happening on the field. Similarly, at school, if a teacher is the one telling students what to do and how to do it, students will not have the opportunity to gain confidence as learners, to apply the skills and strategies they've practiced to new situations, to be flexible and innovative, and to learn from their mistakes. And if the principal is the one telling teachers how to teach and monitoring them to ensure compliance, teachers may realize that this is not what they went to college for. We need to coach teachers to be the best they can be, to continue to grow as educators, and to make a positive difference for their students.

I chose to lead as a coach. I believe that through two-way conversations that included self-assessment, self-reflection, and goal setting, coaches empower their players, their students, or their staff. Empowerment should be our ultimate goal as school leaders whether it is for our students or our teachers.

Coaching is more than just being on the sidelines. Coaches make it possible for our students and teachers to be self-directed, collaborative problem-solvers, and creative thinkers. The legendary basketball coach John Wooden once said, "A good coach can change a game. A great coach can change a life." I strived to be a great coach.

Leading with aloha meant:

• Believing that our students and our teachers, through self-assessment, self-reflection, and goal setting, can be empowered to be responsible for their own learning

• Establishing trusting relationships with teachers so the coaching process can support them to continue to grow as educators

• Making time for coaching conversations that helped our teachers to adjust their instruction to empower and engage students in their learning ❋

CONTINUE TO LEARN

"If you're not learning, you're not reaching your true potential."
—Jim Rohn

Science was a subject that was required in school. Most of the time, we read a textbook, maybe listened to a lecture from the teacher, and then took a test to see how much we remembered. Occasionally, we had a hands-on activity or conducted an experiment, but primarily, we learned science by reading about it. Unfortunately, I retained very little of what I read, and when I became a teacher, I hoped to change that for my students. At a professional development session in the beginning of my career, the speaker wrote five words on the board. Teachers teach science to students. He asked us to change the order of those five words to completely change the meaning of the sentence. I was so excited when I figured it out: Teachers teach students to science. "Science is a verb," the speaker shared. From then on, I made a conscious decision to provide my students (and my sons) with lots of opportunities to science.

We put on our boots and raincoats and took walks in the rain to observe the flow of water and listen to the rhythmic pitter-patter of raindrops on our umbrella. We observed quietly as a spider spun a web then went back the next day to discover her wrapping an unsuspecting insect that was trapped and couldn't escape. We discovered properties of magnets by experimenting with different types of materials. We picked little yellow flowers when we went on a walk, placed them in a vase, and were delighted a few days later to discover they were dandelions. We found tiny eggs laid in holes in the trunk of palm trees and carefully removed them, placed them in a small container padded with Kleenex, and waited. Imagine our surprise when baby lizards hatched from those eggs!

LEARNING TO IMPROVE OUR PRACTICES

But learning is not just about sciencing. Learning is personal. Learning is about applying skills to real-life situations. Learning is about passion for a topic, being curious, asking questions, and seeking answers to take new knowledge to a higher level. Life provides us with so many opportunities to explore, discover, and make sense of new skills or information. Learning is not something that is done only in school. Part of our challenge as educators is to guide students so they can be curious, self-directed, and enthusiastic learners wherever they are. We want students who have the skills and strategies to make a difference for themselves and for others not just now, but in the future as well.

Research on effective teaching and learning practices as well as the advancement of technology have changed teaching and learning. We know that teacher and student collaboration, asking questions and discovering answers through researching, inclusive classrooms, social–emotional learning, problem-solving, and project-based or multi-disciplinary learning are more effective strategies for engaging and empowering students. Teachers are constantly learning through professional development classes, collaborating with their colleagues, analyzing data about whether their students are applying what they learned, observing other teachers teach, and reflecting on their own teaching practices. Much of this learning takes place on their own time—after school, on weekends, or during breaks. Teachers do it because they know it is important that they be the best they can for their students.

As educators, we have a responsibility to not only excite our students about what they are learning; we also need to keep learning ourselves. We are tasked with perhaps the most important job—preparing our students for their future. Educators can't sit back and rely on the same recycled lessons year after year. Today's students are different; they have so many more opportunities to connect, not just within their classroom, but globally as well. Teaching is no longer about helping students to score well on a test; it's about helping students discover a passion for learning and for making a difference, not just for themselves, but for others.

LEARNING AS A PRINCIPAL

When I began my career 45 years ago, I could not have anticipated the changes in our world that have impacted how we teach and learn. In those days, we learned primarily by reading books or by talking with other teachers or attending workshops or conferences. Today, educators have so many more opportunities to continue their learning, both individually and with their colleagues. Just like their students, teachers are much more engaged in their own learning when given voice and choice about their own professional growth. At the school level, teachers need time to dialogue and learn from each other; we must provide the time and the opportunity for them to do so.

When I became a principal, there was so much I had to learn about leading a school and supporting our staff so they could be the best they could be for our students and our school community. I also had to demonstrate that I was a lifelong learner. Fortunately, I had wonderful mentors who took me under their wing and helped me to navigate all of the tasks I was responsible for. I also had a great staff who welcomed me and helped me to understand the strengths and challenges so we could create our shared vision for our school.

I realized that continuing to learn and improve as a school leader would be a priority for me. I wanted to be the leader that our students, staff, and school community deserved. I did a lot of reading and took ideas that I thought would work for me. I joined Twitter where so many educators are sharing ideas and resources, and I realized its impact on my professional learning. I started writing a blog, and although I was initially reluctant to share my ideas publicly, I persevered. I never thought of myself as a writer, but after six years of blogging, I realized that I did have something to share. This experience gave me the courage to write this book.

Technology has been a game changer in education. I adhere to the philosophy that if we use technology, it should make our work more efficient and provide opportunities for students to explore, discover, create, and share. I admit that learning new tech tools was sometimes a challenge for me, but fortunately, our tech team was accommodating and helpful. They patiently took me through the process and encouraged me when I was frustrated. Like our students, I realized that having a positive attitude about learning is essential, and I kept plugging away. I know that today's students are much more comfortable using technology than I could ever be; that is as it should be. This is their world, and they will be the ones who will make a difference using technology.

When I first became a principal, we had one tech lab with 20 computers that had not been replaced in a number of years. From that beginning, we expanded, and now, universal screening is done online and teachers have instant access to their student data; attendance and report cards are submitted online; classroom teachers regularly update their websites or blogs so parents are informed about what is going on in their classrooms; teachers and students are sharing or participating in global projects; and we share files, collaborate on projects, and communicate with others via technology.

This wouldn't have happened without trust and positive relationship-building. It is easy to say that things are going satisfactorily so "why change?" However, as school leaders, we need to be open to learning new ways to be more efficient and transparent. There are more expectations on schools today, and it makes sense to have systems in place which save time and increase collaboration and communication.

As a school leader, I depended on my staff to keep me updated and to be a continuous learner. I encouraged them to keep learning and to keep sharing with others so we can all benefit. As I reflect on my 45 years as an educator, I realize that I was so fortunate to have had so many teachers—my colleagues, our staff, our students, our school community, and my personal global network. All of them helped to mold me into the educator and leader I strived to be.

Leading with aloha meant:

• Continuously learning and encouraging others in our school community to do the same

• Supporting teachers by providing time to explore topics of interest as well as a venue to share their learning with their colleagues

• Being an active member in my professional community by sharing my ideas and learning from others

• Understanding that we can learn from anyone, anywhere, anytime ✿

PART THREE

THE ROAD AHEAD

"Often when you think you're at the end of something,
you're at the beginning of something else."

—*Fred Rogers*

I had decided to retire at the end of the 2017–2018 school year. Once I made my decision, I felt very comfortable. I had been preparing for my pending retirement, and I was confident that the transition to new leadership at our school would be a smooth one. I believed that we were moving in the right direction, that our teachers and students were empowered to truly make a difference in this world, and that although our test scores were not the highest, our students were gaining skills that would help them be successful in their future. But even the best-laid plans could not prepare me for what was to come.

Remembering How He Lived

In January 2018, our second son, Jarand, had spent five days in the hospital in Hawai'i when he was home for a vacation. He had an appointment with his optometrist, and she was alarmed that his eyes were hemorrhaging. She immediately sent him to the emergency room, and after a battery of tests, Jarand was diagnosed with Stage 5 chronic kidney disease. The cause was untreated high blood pressure. The news sent shockwaves to my whole being; how could this have happened? I was totally ignorant about CKD, but I started to research and ask questions. The only thing we could do was to learn as much as we could and to support Jarand as he changed his lifestyle to deal with the heart and kidney issues. In typical Jarand fashion, he followed doctor's orders, took his blood pressure faithfully and recorded his numbers twice daily, took his medication, ate healthy, and went for long walks. He had been active when he was in Hawai'i, playing tennis, bowling, and golfing, but when he moved to Las Vegas, his physical activity declined as he adjusted to a totally new profession that required different skills than what he was used to. Jarand was upbeat and called us whenever he had an appointment to keep us updated. He went to informational sessions about living with kidney disease and even attended a session on kidney transplants. We were all ready to be tested to see if we would be compatible as a donor for Jarand.

On May 20, 2018, Jarand passed away peacefully in his sleep. He had just spent the previous night with his brother, his nephews, and other friends at a *Pokémon Go* Raid and called to chat with us and let us know that he had an early appointment with a client the next day. When he didn't show up, his boss was concerned; Jarand was always so responsible and would never miss an appointment. Justin and his boss went to Jarand's apartment. Justin said it looked like Jarand was sleeping, but he was already cold. The news of Jarand's passing was so difficult for me to process.

I reflect on what helped us get through the dark days. For me, it was hearing from so many of Jarand's friends, primarily through social media, and realizing how much everyone loved him. They shared remembrances of our son, and it warmed my heart to see the positive impact Jarand had on others. New realtors shared about how much Jarand helped them when they first started. Family and friends reminisced about our son, and we laughed when we heard some of the stories. It was also my own personal memories of Jarand and what made him special—his kind heart and his empathy. I remembered times when he could sense that I was upset and would say just the right thing to get me out of my funk.

I had hoped that Jarand would follow in my footsteps and become a teacher. He had coached Jordan's soccer teams from the time he was 12 years old, and he was a great coach. He was positive, organized, taught skills and strategies, and made sure the players had fun, showed good sportsmanship, respected the game, and improved as soccer players. Jarand continued to coach or help out teams throughout his years in high school and at the University of Hawai'i, even while playing competitive tennis. I encouraged Jarand to go into education, but he chose to obtain his degree in history instead. I was so disappointed when he told me that he was tired of going to school and did not want to pursue his master's degree in education.

About three years before his passing, Jarand decided to leave his job here in Hawai'i and move to Las Vegas. Justin had recently gone through a divorce, and Jarand wanted to be there to help him out. He also wanted to share his love for soccer by helping his brother coach Jace and Jayden's teams. Jarand loved waking up early to watch soccer games on TV, and he was thrilled that Jace would often join him, discussing what was happening on the field. Jarand was everyone's favorite uncle, often going over to his friends' homes just to play with their children. He loved winning stuffed animals at arcades and giving them to his friends' kids or his nephews.

Very few people knew that Jarand had applied to be a substitute teacher at Clark County School District. He was looking for a part-time job to supplement his realtor income, and I casually suggested that substitute teaching might be a good option. Again, in typical Jarand fashion, he took action immediately and seemed genuinely excited about the possibility. I thought it was somewhat ironic that just as I was retiring, he was going to experience what it was like to be a teacher. I held out hope that he might even decide to go back to school to become a teacher and do real estate as his side job. Sadly, it was not to be.

Jarand impacted so many people in the 38 years of his life. Although I mourn his passing, I choose to remember how he lived. We realize that Jarand is no longer here with us physically, but his legacy lives on.

TAKE CARE OF YOURSELF

On July 11, 2018, the Honolulu City Council unanimously approved Resolution 18-134 to name the tennis complex at the Patsy T. Mink Central O'ahu Regional Park after our second son. We are humbled by this honor; this 20-court world-class facility hosts national as well as local tournaments, and it is well-utilized throughout the year by players of all ages. On October 21, 2018, we held a formal dedication for the official naming of the Jarand M. Y. Iwase Tennis Complex. This event combined Jarand's love for tennis with a clinic for players young and old as well as screenings by the National Kidney Foundation of Hawai'i. Since Jarand's passing, Randy and I are spreading awareness of chronic kidney disease and the need to take better care of ourselves.

Jarand's unexpected passing made me realize that life is fragile and that we need to take care of ourselves first so we can take care of others. In our busy world, we often put our children or our family or our job first and take care of ourselves only if there is time. Too often, we schedule our kids with multiple activities such as sports or dance or tutoring, leaving us exhausted and running from one activity to the next. This may mean rushing to get dinner started or picking up fast food if it's getting late. The kids are grouchy because they still have homework to do, and parents are annoyed with the kids for grumbling. Let's take a deep breath and really reflect on how we're spending our time.

Retirement has allowed me the opportunity to reflect on all I've accomplished and to ponder what more I want to do with the rest of my life. When I was working, I didn't realize how much of my waking hours were spent on job-related activities. I loved working, and the school staff was like a second family to me. However, now that I have retired, I realize that work consumed my waking hours, even on the weekends or during breaks or while on vacation.

Looking to the Future

Now as I take our dog on his daily walk around the neighborhood, I reminisce. At home, I take out the photo albums or I browse through the plastic bins filled with their work—journals, stories they wrote, pictures they drew—and I realize how proud I am of all my sons.

Jordan's six-year commitment to the Air Force is over, and he is planning for his future. I am proud of how much he has grown through his military experience. Every time I speak with him, I am reassured that he has thought things through and is prepared. He has matured by having to be independent and away from the comforts of home, deploying for six months to the Middle East, and knowing that he was responsible to make the most of his military training. Now that he has returned to Hawaiʻi, he will complete his college degree via the GI Bill, and after that, we will see what the future holds for him.

When Justin told us he was moving his family to Las Vegas, Jace was three years old, and Jayden was one. I was heartbroken; we had gotten so used to seeing them at least once a week when they came over for Sunday dinner, and I already looked forward to watching our grandsons play soccer, or tennis, or golf, or whatever sport they wanted to play. I loved reading books, singing songs, and going for walks with them. Unfortunately, the cost of living in Hawaiʻi made purchasing a home unaffordable for them, and the opportunity to own a house in Las Vegas was too good to pass up. Justin was determined; he worked hard and today, he is a successful realtor. As a dad, he shares his love of learning with his sons, and they have had opportunities that would not be available in Hawaiʻi. A spur-of-the-moment decision could find them getting in the car or taking a short plane trip to go to a professional baseball or football game. They've gone on all-day trips to one of the many national parks nearby. Justin is a great cook and rarely uses a recipe, and Jayden loves to learn from his dad. We are especially grateful to Justin for helping Jarand to acclimate to his new home when he decided to move to Las Vegas. Justin is adventurous and makes the most of his opportunities, and having him there to help his brother find his footing was so important.

Randy retired at the end of 2018, so we will have time to work on projects around the house. We aren't in any hurry, though it would be nice to be done sooner rather than later. We can travel without worrying about what's happening back at work. We can spend more time with our grandsons, our sons, my mom, and the rest of our families, as well as our friends. We may get involved in some volunteer work, and we can think about how we want to spend our free time and what more we want to explore and discover. I look forward to the road ahead. ✤

ABOUT THE AUTHOR

Jan Iwase is a lifelong resident of Hawai'i, who grew up in a pine-apple plantation village on the island of O'ahu and graduated from the University of Hawai'i at Mānoa. In 2002, after teaching in the Head Start program and in the State Department of Education (DOE), she was named principal of Hale Kula Elementary School, later renamed the Daniel K. Inouye Elementary School. She was chosen as the DOE's Central District Elementary Principal of the Year in 2013 and was nominated for the Masayuki Tokioka Excellence in School Leadership award in 2016. Jan retired as principal in 2018 after 45 years as an educator, and today lives in Mililani with her husband, Randy. She is the mother of three sons, Justin, Jarand, and Jordan.